"Emily takes raw foodism to new levels that wow us every single time."
—SIVAN PARDO RENWICK, founder of the blog The Vegan Woman

"Imaginative and inspiring—Emily has upped the bar on raw cuisine."
—MÉRIDIAN ANDERSON, Vegan Secret Supper Chef and author
of *Vegan Secret Supper*

"Emily presents stunning dishes in a way that makes me feel confident
I can just dive right in to raw cuisine."
—BRIAN L. PATTON, author of *The Sexy Vegan Cookbook* and
The Sexy Vegan's Happy Hour at Home

"We really enjoy Emily's fresh approach to raw foods. Her recipes are
simple, but delicious, her writing is casual and inspiring, and her
photographs are simply stunning!"
—MATT & JANABAI AMSDEN, authors of *The Rawvolution Continues*

"Emily's food is simply sublime. With this book, I can wow my friends
with gorgeously tasty, healthy treats!"
—SAMANTHA GOULD, co-editor of *Vegan Food* magazine

rawsome vegan baking

AN UN-COOKBOOK FOR RAW, GLUTEN-FREE, VEGAN, BEAUTIFUL AND
SINFULLY SWEET COOKIES, CAKES, BARS AND CUPCAKES

Emily von Euw

FOUNDER OF THISRAWSOMEVEGANLIFE.COM

PAGE STREET
PUBLISHING CO.

PAGE STREET
PUBLISHING CO.

First published in 2014 by
Page Street Publishing Co.
27 Congress Street, Suite 103
Salem, MA 01970
www.pagestreetpublishing.com

Distributed by Macmillan; sales in Canada by The Canadian Manda Group; distribution
in Canada by The Jaguar Book Group.

17   16   15   14   2   3   4   5   6

ISBN-13: 978-1-62414-055-6
ISBN-10: 1-62414-055-6

Library of Congress Control Number: 2013915133

Cover and book design by Page Street Publishing Co.
Photography by Emily von Euw

Printed and bound in U.S.A.

Page Street is proud to be a member of 1% for the Planet. Members donate one
percent of their sales to one or more of the over 1,500 environmental and
sustainability charities across the globe who participate in this program.

Dedicated to You.

Contents

Introduction

About Me

Who wrote all these words? Who took all these photos? Who made all these desserts? Hey there, sexy—I did. My name is Emily von Euw, and I am very pleased to meet you. I have my own food blog, This Rawsome Vegan Life, where I create, photograph and share raw and vegan recipes with the world, while giving my personal insights and thoughts about my experiences with the lifestyle. People seem to like what I have to offer and that is why you are reading this book. Bam.

I believe that to sustain happiness, you need to have health; it's the foundation for a long, rich life. How can you enjoy anything to the fullest when you don't feel you are functioning at your optimal? Thus ultimately my mission is to spread happiness through healthy eating. I also happen to be vegan because I feel that we are able to make the most of this life when we bring about as much joy as possible, while minimizing suffering for others. However, I understand that everyone is different, and we all must walk our own paths, so I do not judge people based on what they eat. The best diet is the one that makes you feel the happiest and strongest. For me, this ends up being a vegan, predominantly raw one.

Why Raw Vegan?

A whole-foods, plant-based diet has been proven in countless peer-reviewed studies and personal experiences to be excellent for long-term health, and the best lifestyle choice for the planet and certainly our animal friends. I recommend reading *The China Study*, *Mad Cowboy* and *The Food Revolution* to learn more on this. In many cases, cooking and refining our food can destroy much of the vital nutrition we need to thrive. Fruits, vegetables, nuts and seeds are often most nutritious in their raw, whole state. They are able to retain the most vitamins, minerals, enzymes and phytonutrients, which all play major roles in sustainable wellness and a happy, long life. There's an abundance of evidence to show that eating a whole-foods, vegan diet with plenty of raw food is the optimal way of eating for most individuals; but I think the best way to decide what kind of diet is best for you is to experiment and find what makes you happiest. Personally, I feel my best (and happiest) when eating this way.

Raw Food Basics

They're basic. No, seriously—there's really not too much you need to know about the ins and outs of creating raw vegan cuisine; after reading this chapter, essentially you will know all the necessary info. I'm yearnin' for some learnin'—let's go.

What is in raw vegan desserts? Nuts, seeds, fruit, coconut, cacao and other superfoods. What's not in them? Dairy, refined sugar, processed flour, eggs, gluten and other junk your body doesn't need. One thing I love about this way of eating is that everything is simplified, easier and quicker. No cooking (and not much cleaning) required. For the recipes in this book, you won't ever have to remember to preheat the oven, or cringe at the idea of scrubbing the baking pan clean. Scared of ruining the recipes? No worries. They are all basically foolproof and as long as you can press a food processor or blender on and off and pour things evenly into cake pans, you have nothing to fret about. Yes, I just said *fret*.

For a lot of my recipes, you will see that I ask for raw nuts. I don't specify that they need to be soaked, but I do recommend this step. Soaking nuts in water for about three hours, then thoroughly rinsing them, increases their flavor and your body can absorb more nutrients from them. Soaking the nuts also helps make recipes creamier, which is often what you want. It's a time-saving method to buy nuts in bulk, soak them all at once, rinse them and then freeze them. I store all my nuts and seeds in the freezer.

The raw dessert recipes contained in this book all follow a similar pattern; they are made up primarily of fresh fruit, dried fruit, nuts, seeds, coconut and sometimes oats or buckwheat groats. Sounds kind of like a granola bar, right? Well, when you start flipping through the pages, I hope you learn that these wholesome, simple, nutritious ingredients can be transformed into decadent, awe-inspiring, jaw-dropping desserts that will make everyone ask for seconds. I firmly believe that eating healthy doesn't have to mean giving up amazing flavor and indulgence. You should be able to have your cake and eat it too, without one negative thought about your waistline. As I love to say: these recipes allow you to indulge, guilt-free.

Before diving into the recipes after this page, I recommend you flip to the back of the book and look over the Resources chapter (page 212) to learn about ingredients, equipment and substitution options. Knowledge is power!

Finally, all this introduction information is out of the way—on to the fun stuff! Let's party.

chapter 1

Cakes & Cupcakes

EVERYBODY LOVES CAKE. It is a symbol of joyful celebration, special milestones and simply the fun we find in sharing sweet treats made with love with the ones we care for. Cakes and cupcakes are surely my favorite raw dessert to make because they always attract oohs and aahs from my readers and the people I share them with. There's just something about them that makes people straight up giddy. Straight up.

Whenever I make a cake or cupcakes (which is abnormally often), I make sure that I use love as a main ingredient, and take the utmost care when preparing and decorating them. That may sound cheesy, but I honestly think that that extra care makes the recipe taste better. My cakes and cupcakes usually disappear within two or three days, and no—that's not because I am devouring them all by myself, although I probably could.

The cakes and cupcakes you will find in this chapter are perfect for any special occasion, and a surefire way to impress whoever sees them. You don't need to be a pro baker to have success with these recipes either, because there's no baking required. Don't worry about burning the cake, mixing the icing too long or having it all fall apart on you at the last minute. Most of the recipes just require some blending, spreading evenly into a springform pan and then overnight refrigeration. Easy! I have an adjustable cake pan but generally a 9-inch (23 cm) pan will work for the cake recipes. Don't worry, though; they will all turn out delicious, regardless of what diameter they are. The majority of these cakes and cupcakes will last for several days—in fact, a lot of them taste better the second day because it gives them time to develop their flavor.

Cashew Coffee Vanilla Crème Cake with Cinnamon Chocolate Crust

This will get you hyped in the healthiest way.

> Makes: 1 cake, 10 servings

CASHEW COFFEE VANILLA CRÈME
2 cups (290 g) raw cashews
Seeds from 1 vanilla pod
3 tablespoons (44 ml) melted coconut oil
1/4 cup (85 g) pure maple syrup
1/8 teaspoon salt
1/3 cup (79 ml) strong brewed coffee

CINNAMON CHOCOLATE CRUST
1 cup (100 g) raw pecans
1 cup (175 g) pitted dates
2 tablespoons (15 g) cacao powder
1/8 teaspoon salt
1/4 teaspoon ground cinnamon

SALTED CARAMEL DRIZZLE
1/2 cup (88 g) pitted dates, soaked in water or coffee for 30 minutes
1/2 teaspoon salt
1 tablespoon (16 g) raw nut butter (optional)

GARNISH
Coffee beans
Goji berries
Raw pumpkin seeds

TO MAKE THE CRÈME: Blend all the ingredients until smooth. Set aside.

TO MAKE THE CRUST: Pulse the nuts into a coarse flour in your food processor and add all the other ingredients until you can press it together, and then press it into the bottom of a parchment paper–lined small springform pan (mine is 4 1/2 inches [11.5 cm] in diameter). Scoop the crème on top of the crust and let it set in the fridge or freezer.

TO MAKE THE CARAMEL DRIZZLE: Blend the dates, their soaking liquid and the salt and nut butter (if using) until smooth and pretty liquid. If it is too thick, add more water; if too thin, add more dates. Drizzle on top of your crème cake and garnish with coffee beans, goji berries and pumpkin seeds. It is better—but difficult—to wait until the next day to eat this, to let the flavors get to know one another. Then *devour.*

Super Sexy Cacao Cashew Cupcakes

These are big, and they're bodacious. They differ slightly from my other chocolate nut butter cup recipe (page 98) in that they aren't made up solely of raw chocolate and nut butter; they have a chocolate crust encasing cashew butter, and more of a chocolate cream on top. You decide which one you prefer (if you can actually choose). Oh, and as always, use whatever nut butter you like; I just favored cashew the day I made these.

> Makes: 4 very large cupcakes

CRUST
1 cup (145 g) raw almonds
1 cup (175 g) pitted dates
1 tablespoon (7 g) cacao powder

FILLING
4 tablespoons (64 g) raw cashew butter

CHOCOLATE CREAM
1½ tablespoons (22 ml) melted coconut oil
1½ tablespoons (22 g) cacao powder
1½ tablespoons (30 g) agave nectar

TO MAKE THE CRUST: Process the almonds into flour in your food processor, and then add the dates and cacao and process until it begins to stick together. Press into four cupcake tins and put in the fridge.

TO MAKE THE CHOCOLATE CREAM: Mix together all the ingredients until smooth. Scoop a tablespoon of cashew butter into each crust, followed by the chocolate cream mixture. Put back in the fridge for 1 hour, then destroy them with your mouth! Rawr!

Buckwheat & Berry Cream Cake

When I made this recipe the first time, the white layer of the cake was too thin, so I decided I'd add some oat flour to thicken it up, but I found that I had run out. Instead I used buckwheat flour and discovered that I actually preferred the flavor with the addition of the buckwheat! I could have named this recipe something else but I think that buckwheat deserves some recognition. It's a superfood with a special flavor all its own. Note: The crust is optional but nice for another texture (if you want to keep the amount of nuts low, simply use oats or buckwheat groats instead of almonds).

> Makes: 1 cake, 9 to 12 servings

CRUST
1 cup (145 g) raw almonds
1½ cups (263 g) pitted dates
Pinch of salt (optional)

BUCKWHEAT LAYER
2 cups (290 g) raw cashews
1 cup (120 g) buckwheat flour
1 cup (236 ml) coconut milk, or as needed
¼ cup (59 ml) melted coconut oil
¼ cup (85 g) preferred liquid sweetener

BERRY LAYER
3 cups (765 g) frozen cherries
¼ cup (59 ml) coconut oil
1 cup (175 g) pitted dates
¾ cup (177 ml) coconut milk, or as needed

TO MAKE THE CRUST: Pulse the almonds into flour in your food processor. Add the dates and salt (if using) and process until it gets sticky. Press into the bottom of a parchment paper–lined springform pan. Put in the fridge.

TO MAKE THE BUCKWHEAT LAYER: Blend the ingredients together until very smooth and thick, using as little coconut milk as possible. Spread the buckwheat mixture onto your crust.

TO MAKE THE BERRY LAYER: Combine the ingredients, then pour the berry mixture on top of the buckwheat layer. Refrigerate or freeze overnight until the cake is solid.

Neapolitan Mousse Cake

This is an extremely easy recipe. As long as you have a blender or food processor, you don't need any skills besides a working finger to press on and off. My dad said this recipe looked like a giant cupcake, and I don't think that's a bad thing at all. It's pretty girly and fairy tale-looking so you'd be a popular penguin—so to speak, I am pretty sure you would not actually transform into a penguin—if you served this at a tea party or girls' night . . . that sort of thing.

> Makes: 1 cake, 8 servings

CHOCOLATE LAYER
1 ripe avocado, peeled and pitted

1 cup (175 g) pitted dates

1 tablespoon (7 g) cacao powder

1 teaspoon vanilla extract

VANILLA LAYER
3/4 cup (109 g) raw cashews

2 tablespoons (40 g) pure maple syrup

1 tablespoon (15 ml) melted coconut oil

2 tablespoons (30 ml) water, or as needed

STRAWBERRY LAYER
1/2 cup (83 g) raw almonds

1 teaspoon vanilla extract

1 cup (145 g) hulled fresh strawberries

1 tablespoon (20 g) pure maple syrup (optional)

TOPPING (OPTIONAL)
Chopped raw almonds

Cacao nibs

Goji berries

Line a small springform pan (mine is 4 1/2 inches [11.5 cm] in diameter) with parchment paper and set it aside. For each layer, simply blend the ingredients until smooth and thick, and layer evenly in your pan (in whatever order you like). Refrigerate overnight. Top off with chopped almonds, cacao nibs and goji berries, if desired.

Rawified Reese's Ice-Cream Cake

Oh. My. Gosh. This is a new all-time favorite. The rich creaminess of the peanut butter and chocolate combination is simply unbeatable. Here is one indulgence you can feel great about enjoying. I think this recipe would be 100 percent perfect for absolutely any occasion. Every person you give a piece to will love you forever, and I cannot think of a situation where that would ever be a bad thing. Make this now. You can use whatever nut butter you prefer.

> Makes: 1 cake, 8 servings

CAKE

2 cups (290 g) raw cashews

1 banana

1/4 cup (30 g) cacao powder

2 1/2 tablespoons (50 g) pure maple syrup (optional)

1 cup (175 g) pitted dates

About 1/2 cup (118 ml) water, or as needed

1 teaspoon vanilla extract

1/4 cup (59 ml) melted coconut oil

TOPPING

3 tablespoons (45 ml) raw chocolate in liquid form (see page 209)

3 tablespoons (48 g) raw peanut butter

3 large chocolate peanut butter cups (see page 98)

8 small peanut butter cups (see page 98)

MAKE THE CAKE: Blend all the cake ingredients until smooth and very thick, using as little water as possible. Spread evenly into a springform pan and then swirl in the liquid chocolate and peanut butter on top. Put in the freezer overnight, or you can keep it in the fridge for a softer texture. The next day, decorate with peanut butter cups and devour the chocolate beast.

Black Forest Cake

I'm reppin' my German heritage with this one. Be sure to let your frosting thicken up in the fridge prior to using it, otherwise you will have a messy situation on your hands. Also, I recommend buying a bar of raw chocolate, or simply use dark chocolate for the chocolate shavings because the homemade version will probably be too soft. You can use whatever kind of cherries you like.

> Makes: 1 cake, about 4 servings

CAKE
1 cup (100 g) raw pecans
1½ cups (263 g) pitted dates
1 tablespoon (7 g) cacao powder
½ teaspoon vanilla extract
Pinch of salt

FROSTING
1¾ cups (254 g) raw cashews
⅓ cup (79 ml) coconut milk
¼ cup (59 ml) coconut oil
¼ cup (85 g) preferred liquid sweetener

DECORATIONS
Handful of cherries
Raw/dark chocolate shavings

TO MAKE THE CAKE: Pulse the pecans into flour in your food processor. Add the rest of the ingredients and process until it begins to stick together like dough. Press into your largest cookie cutter molds, essentially forming your cake layers. I was able to make two layers. Put these in your fridge to set.

TO MAKE THE FROSTING: Blend all the ingredients until smooth and fairly thick. It will thicken more once you put it in the fridge . . . so put it in the fridge for 1 to 2 hours. Once it's thick enough to frost with, spread it evenly over the top of your first cake layer. Put the second layer on top and repeat. If you only made two layers, frost the sides as well. Otherwise, continue adding your layers until you don't have any more, and then frost the sides.

Put in the fridge overnight, or eat right away if you just can't wait. Before serving, decorate with cherries and chocolate shavings. Woo!

Vanilla Chocolate Chunk Cheesecake with Peanut Butter

One of the best things I have ever put in my mouth.

> Makes: 1 cake, 8 to 10 servings

CRUST
1 cup (90 g) oats
1 cup (175 g) pitted dates

CHEESECAKE
2 bananas
1/4 cup (59 ml) melted coconut oil
2 cups (190 g) raw cashews
1 1/2 cups (263 g) pitted dates
1/4 cup (85 g) preferred liquid sweetener (optional)
Seeds from 1 vanilla pod
Water
1/4 cup (30 g) cacao or carob powder

TOPPING
3 tablespoons (48 g) raw peanut butter
3 tablespoons (18 g) raw chocolate (see page 209)

TO MAKE THE CRUST: Pulse the oats into flour in your food processor, and then add the dates and process until they stick together. Press into the bottom of a springform pan and put in the fridge.

TO MAKE THE CHEESECAKE: Blend all ingredients, except the cacao powder, until very smooth, using as little water as possible, to keep your cheesecake creamy. If you don't want to add any water, use some liquid sweetener or another banana. This is your vanilla layer. Transfer half of the batter to a bowl. To make the chocolate layer, add the cacao powder to the remaining batter that is still in your blender and blend until it's incorporated. Now spread the vanilla layer and the chocolate layer on your crust, alternating layers a few times. Set in the freezer overnight and then drizzle with peanut butter and chocolate the next day. Enjoy!

Strawberry Banana Cream Cake with Mint

This was actually quite easy to make and it didn't take much time, not including freezing. It may appear plain on the outside—unless you decorate with berries, mint and chocolate—but when you cut it open, there's that burst of pink! My fave color. If you have a fear of pink (umm . . .), just use blueberries instead of strawberries. Problem solved.

> Makes: 1 cake, 8 servings

PINK FILLING
3 bananas
2 cups (510 g) frozen strawberries (or other berries)
1 to 3 tablespoons (15 to 45 ml) coconut oil

CREAM LAYER
2 cups (290 g) raw cashews
2 cups (350 g) pitted dates
1 orange, peeled and seeded
2 tablespoons (30 ml) melted coconut oil
Water

Mint for garnish

TO MAKE THE PINK FILLING: Put the bananas into your blender, followed by the frozen berries and blend until smooth. Spread evenly into a springform pan—this pan should be slightly smaller than the second one you will use. I have an adjustable one so I simply made it smaller for this layer, and then widened it for the second part. If you don't have either of those options, don't worry. The bottom part can be pink and you can just add the cream layer on top. Freeze until solid, about 3 hours.

TO MAKE THE CREAM LAYER: Blend all ingredients until smooth, using as little water as possible, if you need any at all. The less water you use, the creamier it will be. Using a larger-diameter springform pan, place the frozen pink layer inside and then spread the cream layer around the sides and top. Or you can use the same pan and spread the cream only on top. Freeze until solid for about 3 hours or overnight, and then garnish with mint, slice and enjoy! Store in the freezer.

Nut-free Creamy Coconut Cheesecake

You're gonna love my *lack* of nuts . . . in this recipe (I really hope you got that reference). To be honest, I prefer this recipe to some nut-based cheesecake recipes. It's exceptionally silky smooth and I frankly cannot resist coconut. This cheesecake leaves nothing to be desired . . . except maybe a second slice. Serve with fruit, if you like, and double or triple the recipe for a larger cake.

> Makes: 1 small cake, 5 to 7 servings

CRUST
1/2 cup (45 g) oats or (85 g) buckwheat groats
1/2 cup (88 g) pitted dates

CHEESECAKE
3/4 cup (60 g) fresh young coconut meat
1/4 cup (59 ml) liquid coconut oil
2 1/2 tablespoons (50 g) preferred liquid sweetener, or to taste
1/3 cup (29 g) unsweetened shredded coconut
Juice of 1 lemon

TO MAKE THE CRUST: Pulse the oats into flour in your food processor, then add the dates and process until it all begins to stick together in crumbs. Press into the bottom of a small springform pan (mine is 4 1/2 inches [11.5 cm] in diameter).

TO MAKE THE CHEESECAKE: Blend all the ingredients until smooth. Pour onto your crust and refrigerate overnight so it can set and develop flavor. The next day it should be solid and ready to chow down on!

Chocolate Cheesecake with Chocolate Chile Drizzle

Oh my lusciousness. This one is a real treat because the ingredients add up pretty high, but I mean, who needs money when you have raw chocolate cake? C'mon. Priorities. But if you don't have a party of people to feed and wanna be cool and frugal, you can halve the recipe.

> Makes: 1 cake, 10 to 12 servings

CRUST
1 cup (90 g) oats
1 cup (175 g) pitted dates

CAKE
1 cup (175 g) pitted dates
2 cups (290 g) raw cashews
2 cups (160 g) fresh young coconut meat
1 cup (236 ml) coconut water
1 cup (236 ml) melted coconut oil
1/4 cup (85 g) preferred liquid sweetener
1/3 cup (40 g) cacao powder
1 teaspoon vanilla extract
1 teaspoon chili powder (more or less as desired)

DRIZZLE
1 tablespoon (20 g) preferred liquid sweetener
1 tablespoon (7 g) cacao powder
2 tablespoons (30 ml) melted coconut oil or cacao butter
Chili powder
Pinch of salt (optional)

TO MAKE THE CRUST: Pulse the oats into flour in your food processor, then add the dates and process until it all sticks together. Press into the bottom of a parchment paper-lined springform pan and refrigerate until you spread on the cake mixture.

TO MAKE THE CAKE: Blend all the ingredients until smooth. It will be very thick so if your blender needs a break, let it take one. Once the texture and taste is to your liking, pour onto your crust and refrigerate for 48 hours to let it develop its flavor and set properly.

Make the drizzle right before serving by mixing together all the ingredients until smooth, adding chili powder as desired. Once ready to serve, slice and drizzle with the drizzle.

Mini Beet Mousse Cakes with Sweet Cashew Cream & Spiced Nuts

If you like the taste of beets, you will love this recipe. The fresh, earthy flavor from them pairs wonderfully with the sweet cashew cream. The spiced nuts on top add another texture and warm flavor component. This would be delicious served with coconut ice cream at any time of year.

> Makes: 2 towers, 4 servings

RED VELVET MOUSSE
1 beet, peeled and thinly sliced on a mandoline
⅓ cup (59 g) pitted dates
⅓ cup (32 g) almond flour
1 tablespoon (15 ml) coconut oil (optional)

CASHEW CREAM
½ cup (73 g) raw cashews
Juice of 1 lemon
¼ cup (44 g) pitted dates, or 1 tablespoon (20 g) pure maple syrup
1 tablespoon (15 ml) coconut oil
2½ tablespoons (39 ml) water, or as needed

SPICED CASHEWS
2 tablespoons (18 g) chopped raw cashews
1 teaspoon pure maple syrup
⅛ teaspoon ground cinnamon
⅛ teaspoon ground cloves
⅛ teaspoon ground nutmeg

TO MAKE THE MOUSSE: Reserve four slices of beet for layering later. Blend the remaining beets, dates and flour until smooth and thick (like pudding). If it is not thick enough, add more dates or flour.

TO MAKE THE CASHEW CREAM: Blend all the ingredients until smooth and thick, adding water as needed.

TO MAKE THE SPICED CASHEWS: Mix the maple syrup and spices with the chopped nuts until evenly coated. Put in a dehydrator for a few hours, until they are crunchy.

ASSEMBLY: Use a cookie cutter (about 3 inches in diameter, a simple circle shape) to cut the reserved beet slices. Now they will fit in your mold perfectly. Now place the cookie cutter mold on parchment paper, and line the inside with parchment paper, making sure it's cut tall enough for your tower (2 to 3 inches [5 to 7.5 cm]). Layer the inside with the mousse, cashew cream, a beet slice, more cashew cream, another beet slice, more cashew cream and finally the mousse again. You should have enough for two towers. Put them in the fridge or freezer for a few hours to let them set, then sprinkle with the spiced nuts and enjoy!

Rainbow Cake with Coconut Banana Cream & Fruit Layers

This cake is glorious! We are naturally drawn toward bright colors and I wanted to show that by focusing on vibrantly colored fresh fruits in this recipe. It's basically a pile of fruit wrapped in coconut banana cream. Mmm . . . as it's mostly fresh fruit, try to eat the cake within a few days of making it.

> Makes: 1 cake, 5 to 10 servings

COCONUT BANANA CREAM

2 bananas

2 cups (473 ml) coconut cream (page 207)

$1/4$ cup (63 g) raw sugar

FRUIT LAYERS

2 cups (290 g) blueberries

2 cups (356 g) peeled and sliced kiwi (sliced about $3/8$ inch [1 cm] thick)

2 cups (330 g) peeled, pitted and sliced mango (sliced about $3/8$ inch [1 cm] thick)

2 cups (340 g) hulled and sliced strawberries (sliced about $3/8$ inch [1 cm] thick)

Additional berries, for garnish

Fresh mint leaves, for garnish

TO MAKE THE CREAM: Blend the bananas until smooth. Put them, the coconut cream and the sugar in a mixing bowl and whisk until stiff peaks form, or it thickens enough to use as frosting.

ASSEMBLY: In a springform pan, drop in the blueberries, then spread on as little frosting as possible in a thin later. Repeat with the other fruits in the order they're listed. Remove the pan and carefully frost the sides. Decorate with berries and mint leaves. Let it set in the fridge for a few hours, then enjoy!

S'mores Cupcakes

Rich, sweet and countless times more nutritious that its gelatinous, corn syrup-drenched counterpart, this recipe is sure to please kids and adults alike around the campfire or whatever occasion you make them for.

> Makes: 4 huge cupcakes

CRUST
1 cup (90 g) oats
1 cup (175 g) pitted dates
Pinch of vanilla extract
Pinch of ground cinnamon

CHOCOLATE
3 tablespoons (23 g) cacao powder
3 tablespoons (45 ml) melted coconut oil
2 tablespoons (40 g) preferred liquid sweetener

MARSHMALLOW LAYER
1 cup (145 g) raw cashews
¼ cup (59 ml) coconut milk
¼ cup (59 ml) coconut oil
2 tablespoons (40 g) preferred liquid sweetener

TO MAKE THE CRUST: Process the oats into powder in your food processor. Add the rest of the ingredients and process until it all sticks together. Press into cupcake tins and put in the fridge.

TO MAKE THE CHOCOLATE: Mix all the ingredients together until smooth. Pour a bit into each crust.

TO MAKE THE MARSHMALLOW LAYER: Blend all the ingredients until smooth and thick. Spread on top of the chocolate and put back in the fridge for a couple of hours.

Chocolate Molten Lava Cakes with Goji Berries

This is still an all-time favorite on my blog, and I can't say I'm surprised. Just look at the gooey chocolate goodness. Can YOU resist?

> Makes: about 4 large lava cakes

CAKE
⅓ cup (30 g) oats
⅓ cup (79 ml) raw walnuts
¼ cup (59 ml) cacao powder
⅓ cup (175 g) pitted dates
⅓ cup (59 g) raisins

MOLTEN LAVA MIDDLE
⅓ cup (79 ml) melted cacao butter
⅓ cup (115 g) pure maple syrup
⅓ cup (59 g) pitted dates
⅓ cup (40 g) cacao powder
¼ teaspoon ground cinnamon
¼ teaspoon Himalayan sea salt
¼ teaspoon chili powder
Vegan milk

Cacao nibs, for garnish
Goji berries, for garnish

TO MAKE THE CAKES: Pulse the oats, walnuts and cacao powder in your food processor until they become a coarse flour. Add the dates and raisins and process until it all starts to stick together. Using about two-thirds of the mixture (you have to save some for the tops), press into the bottom and sides of parchment paper–lined cupcake tins and put in the fridge. Use the rest of the mixture to make the tops by pressing it into cookie molds the same diameter of your cupcake tins. Put those in the fridge as well.

TO MAKE THE MOLTEN MIDDLE: Blend all ingredients until smooth, adding the milk, as needed, to make it creamy and a "molten" consistency (whatever that means . . . hopefully you know). Take the cakes out of the cupcake molds and pour the molten mixture into each one, filling up almost to the top. Now carefully press the tops onto the cakes, gently pressing together the edges. Flip over and decorate with cacao nibs and goji berries. Eat da lava, mohn.

A FEW SUBSTITUTION OPTIONS: To make these gluten-free, use buckwheat groats instead of oats. If you don't want to use cacao, use coconut oil instead of cacao butter and carob instead of cacao powder.

Pink Cherry Ice Cream Cake

I love how this cake looks and tastes; it's girly, it's simple, it's sweet and delicious.

> Makes: 1 cake, 9 servings

FRUIT MOSAIC LAYER

1½ cups (355 ml) coconut cream (page 207)
2 cups (510 g) frozen cherries
Seeds from 1 vanilla pod
¼ cup (85 g) agave nectar

BERRY CREAM LAYER

½ cup (128 g) frozen strawberries
1 cup (134 g) raw macadamia nuts
½ cup (118 ml) coconut milk
½ cup (88 g) pitted dates

TO MAKE THE FRUIT MOSAIC: Blend all the ingredients—except the cherries—until smooth. Pour into a bowl and then drop in the cherries. Set aside.

TO MAKE THE BERRY CREAM: Blend all the ingredients until smooth. Spread into a springform pan, followed by the cherry mixture. Freeze overnight.

Vanilla Herb Cheesecake with Walnut Crust, Rosemary, Orange Mint & Fresh Fruit

This is a delightfully simple dish that would be perfect for a spring or summer dessert, because you can top it off with fresh, local, in-season fruit. The first time I made raw vegan cheesecake, I could hardly believe how delicious it was. It's truly a winning recipe that anyone can enjoy, without the feeling of heaviness and guilt afterward. I think it would be perfect topped with fresh figs and herbs. I used berries and orange mint leaves.

> Makes: 1 cheesecake, 8 to 10 servings

CRUST
1 cup (120 g) raw walnuts
1 cup (175 g) raisins

CHEESECAKE
2 cups (290 g) raw cashews
1 cup (80 g) fresh young coconut meat
½ cup (118 ml) coconut water, or as needed
¼ cup (59 ml) melted coconut oil
3 tablespoons (60 g) preferred liquid sweetener
1 teaspoon vanilla extract
Juice of 1 lemon

TOPPING
Sprig of fresh rosemary and/or orange mint, for garnish
Whatever fruit is in season!

TO MAKE THE CRUST: Process the walnuts and raisins in your food processor until they begin to stick together. Press into the bottom of a springform pan and put in the fridge.

TO MAKE THE CHEESECAKE: Blend all the ingredients until very thick and creamy, using as little coconut water as possible. Spread evenly onto your crust and set in the fridge for 1 to 2 days to let the flavor develop and the cake set. Garnish with your herbs and fruit and enjoy!

Blueberry Strawberry Banana Ice-Cream Cake

This cake was so delicious I couldn't wait for it to completely freeze before I started eating it . . . #YOLO

> Makes: 1 cake, 8 servings

DECORATION
10 strawberries, hulled and cut in half

VANILLA ICE-CREAM CAKE LAYER
2 cups (290 g) raw cashews
2 bananas
1 cup (175 g) pitted dates
1/4 cup (59 ml) melted coconut oil
Seeds from 1 vanilla pod
Vegan milk or coconut water

BERRY LAYER
1 cup (155 g) frozen blueberries
1 cup (255 g) frozen strawberries
1 cup (236 ml) vegan milk or coconut water, or as needed
1 cup (175 g) pitted dates or (100 g) raw walnuts, or another banana

TO MAKE THE FIRST LAYER: Place the halved strawberries around the edge of a springform pan. Set aside. Now blend all the vanilla ice-cream cake ingredients together until smooth, adding as little vegan milk or coconut water as possible (I used about 1/4 cup [59 ml]). Spread into the bottom of the pan; this should press the berries to the inner edge. Put in the freezer.

TO MAKE THE BERRY LAYER: Blend it all up until smooth. Carefully spread over top of the vanilla ice-cream cake layer and put in the freezer for 2 or 3 hours, until it's set. Then cut and serve with other berries! Let it soften a little before eating, because it makes it creamier.

Triple-Threat Chocolate Cake with Avocado Cacao Ganache & Ginger Chocolate Sauce

Unlike a lot of other raw vegan chocolate cake recipes I have seen, this one isn't overloaded with calorically dense nuts (hurray for buckwheat!). I love adding spices such as chile and ginger to chocolate because they enhance the natural flavor and really open up your palate. You create a delectable balance of bitter, spicy and sweet. The original lovers of cacao—the Mayans—paired their chocolate drinks with chile and called it "the food of the gods" . . . mmm, gimme a piece o' dat!

> Makes: 2 to 4 servings

CAKE
1 cup (170 g) buckwheat groats
1 cup (100 g) raw pecans
1 cup (175 g) pitted dates
3 tablespoons (22 g) carob powder

GANACHE
2 avocados
2 tablespoons (30 ml) melted coconut oil
2 tablespoons (40 g) preferred liquid sweetener
2 tablespoons (15 g) cacao powder
1/4 teaspoon chili powder

SAUCE
3 tablespoons (23 g) cacao powder
3 tablespoons (45 ml) melted coconut oil
3 tablespoons (60 g) preferred liquid sweetener
1/4 teaspoon ground ginger

TO MAKE THE CAKE: Process the buckwheat into flour in your food processor, then add the pecans and process the same again. Add the dates and carob and process until it all starts to stick together. Press one-third of this mixture into the bottom of a parchment paper-lined loaf pan, and then gently pull up the lining so the layer of pressed cake comes out in one piece. Set this aside and do it again with half of the remaining mixture. With the rest of your cake mixture, press into the bottom of the pan and leave it there.

TO MAKE THE GANACHE: Blend everything in your food processor until smooth. Spread two-thirds of this onto the layer in the bottom of your pan. Then carefully add one of the layers you have set aside. Repeat. Put in the fridge overnight to set. If you want an ice-cream cake, put it in the freezer (it's also easier to handle when frozen).

TO MAKE THE SAUCE: Mix everything together until smooth and combined. Take out your cake. Separate the cake from the sides of the pan with a knife and then flip the pan over. The cake should fall out but if it doesn't, give the pan a good shake. Now cut your cake into four sections and drizzle each one with your sauce. I stacked two sections on top of each other because more cake = better.

Blueberry Fields Forever Cake with Coconut & Chocolate Avocado Layers

When you make this cake, the blueberry and coconut cream layers look like blueberry-filled clouds—it's a beautiful and dreamy sight so that's where the name of this recipe comes from. In the middle you get a bite of avocado chocolate pudding, which goes oh-so-well with the berries and coconut. Another great one for parties or simply to impress skeptics and nonskeptics alike. It's rainin' cake! Hallelujah!

> Makes: 1 cake, 8 to 10 servings

BLUEBERRY COCONUT LAYER

1 cup (145 g) raw cashews

2 cups (473 ml) coconut cream (page 207)

2 tablespoons (40 g) preferred liquid sweetener

1 teaspoon vanilla extract

4 cups (580 g) blueberries

CHOCOLATE AVOCADO LAYER

2 avocados

2 tablespoons (15 g) cacao powder

2 tablespoons (40 g) preferred liquid sweetener

1/3 cup (79 ml) almond milk, or as needed

TO MAKE THE BLUEBERRY COCONUT LAYER: Blend all the ingredients except the blueberries until smooth. In a tall springform or adjustable pan, pour in half the mixture, as well as 2 cups of the blueberries. Mix together gently so the blueberries are evenly distributed and you get a cool blue and white swirl effect. Freeze until solid.

TO MAKE THE CHOCOLATE LAYER: Blend all the ingredients until smooth and thick, adding almond milk, as needed. Spread this evenly over your bottom blueberry coconut layer of the cake. Freeze until solid, and then pour on the rest of your coconut cream mixture, as well as the remaining 2 cups of blueberries. Mix in the berries evenly, then freeze until solid. Voilà!

Berry Cream Cakes with Chia Pudding

These were a sort of experiment that turned out tasty. Phew! When I began making them, I had something totally different in mind for the finished product, but as fate had it, these are what I ended up with. I'm not complaining! They're the perfect summer treat, especially when frozen.

> Makes: 3 to 4 little cakes

2 cups (510 g) frozen berries

1/2 cup (73 g) raw cashews

1 tablespoon (15 ml) melted coconut oil

Almond milk

3 tablespoons (31 g) chia seeds gelled with 6 tablespoons (90 ml) almond milk

1/2 teaspoon vanilla extract

1 teaspoon preferred liquid sweetener (optional)

1/4 teaspoon green tea powder

Blend the berries, cashews and coconut oil until very thick and creamy, adding as little almond milk as possible. Using half this mixture, pour into the bottom of large cupcake molds and put in the fridge or freezer until set. Next, combine the chia seed mixture with the vanilla and sweetener (if using). Spread this over your berry mixture in the cupcake molds and cover with the remaining berry mixture. Allow to set in the fridge or freezer and then dust with green tea powder for some colorful contrast.

Deep-Dish Chocolate Peanut Butter Ice-Cream Cake

I said it on my blog, when I shared this recipe then, and I will say it again now: *dis cake cray.*

> Makes: 1 honkin' cake, 10 to 12 servings

CRUST
¹/₂ cup (84 g) hemp seeds
¹/₃ cup (56 g) whole flaxseeds
3 tablespoons (23 g) cacao powder
1 cup (175 g) pitted dates

FILLING
3 bananas, frozen
1 cup (175 g) pitted dates
2 cups (290 g) raw cashews
2 tablespoons (30 ml) coconut oil
¹/₄ cup (30 g) cacao powder
1¹/₄ cups (296 ml) water or vegan milk, or as needed
2 tablespoons (32 g) raw peanut butter

Liquid raw chocolate (optional, page 209)
Favorite raw nut butter (optional)

TO MAKE THE CRUST: Pulse the hemp seeds, flaxseeds and cacao in your food processor until they become a coarse flour, then add the dates and process until it all gets sticky. Press into the bottom and up the sides of a springform pan. Put in the fridge.

TO MAKE THE FILLING: Blend all the ingredients until smooth, adding the water, as needed, to make it creamy. Spread evenly into your crust, occasionally swirling in chocolate sauce and nut butter, if you're using them (soooo recommended). Put in the freezer overnight or until frozen solid, and let it thaw a little bit before serving, so it's nice and creamy. Enjoy!

Triple Layer Ice-Cream Cake with Cashew Peppermint, Banana Strawberry & Coconut Vanilla Layers

Obviously this is a recipe made to impress; layers of vibrant colors tend to do that. But it's not just pretty lookin'—it also tastes great. People could literally not stop eating this and for me, that's the best compliment. The flavors are all very refreshing so this a terrific cake to make in the warmer seasons, and I can see it being a huge hit at birthday parties. Let them eat raw vegan ice-cream cake!

> Makes: 1 cake, 10 to 12 servings

CASHEW PEPPERMINT ICE CREAM

2 cups (290 g) raw cashews

½ cup (48 g) firmly packed peppermint leaves

¼ cup (85 g) preferred liquid sweetener

¼ cup (60 ml) melted coconut oil

1 cup (236 ml) almond milk, or as needed

COCONUT VANILLA ICE CREAM

2 cups (473 ml) coconut cream (page 207)

Seeds from 1 vanilla pod

2 tablespoons (40 g) preferred liquid sweetener

1 cup (145 g) raw cashews

BANANA STRAWBERRY ICE CREAM

3 bananas

2 cups (510 g) frozen strawberries (or, if you have frozen bananas, you can use fresh, hulled strawberries)

TO MAKE EACH LAYER: Simply blend all the ingredients in each list separately, until smooth. Put into separate bowls. In a springform or adjustable cake pan, spread on a layer of cashew peppermint ice cream. Put this in the freezer for about 45 minutes, or until it's solid. Next, pour on some coconut vanilla ice cream and freeze until solid. You get the idea. Keep layering on your ice-cream mixtures until you have used them all up and your cake is solid. When you want to serve it, give it some time to thaw and get creamy.

Carrot Cake with Cashew Cream Cheese Frosting

This is the most popular recipe on my blog, and rightly so. It is so sinfully satisfying yet healthy at the same time. The carrot cake is moist and flavorful, while the frosting is creamy and sweet. Ugh, now my mouth is watering. Make it!

> Makes: 1 cake, 8 servings

CASHEW FROSTING

2 cups (290 g) raw cashews, preferably soaked for a couple of hours
1 to 2 tablespoons (15 to 30 ml) freshly squeezed lemon juice
2 tablespoons (30 ml) liquid coconut oil
1/3 cup (115 g) pure maple syrup
Water

CAKE

2 large carrots, peeled
1 1/2 cups (180 g) oat flour
1 cup (175 g) pitted dates
1 cup (145 g) dried pineapple
1/2 cup (43 g) unsweetened shredded coconut
1/2 teaspoon ground cinnamon

TO MAKE THE FROSTING: Blend all the ingredients in your high-speed blender until smooth, using as little water as possible. Taste it—mmm. Transfer to a bowl and set aside.

TO MAKE THE CAKE: Cut the carrots into small chunks. Then throw all the ingredients (including the carrots) in your food processor and pulse until it's all in really small pieces and sticks together.

ASSEMBLY: Press half of the cake mixture into the bottom of an adjustable springform pan (mine was about 6 inches [15 cm] in diameter). Then spread on about one-third of the frosting. Put it in the freezer for 30 to 50 minutes, or until the layer of frosting is hard. Then press on the rest of the cake mix. I let it set in the fridge overnight, and then frosted the whole thing, but you can do it right away, if you want. Take it out of the pan and use the remaining frosting, then cover with whatever garnishes you like. Enjoy!

Double Decadence Chocolate Silk Cake with Hazelnut Crust

It does not get any more decadent.

> Makes: 1 cake, 8 to 10 servings

CRUST
¾ cup (102 g) raw hazelnuts
1 tablespoon (8 g) cacao powder
1 cup (145 g) raisins

CAKE
1 cup (145 g) raw cashews
1 cup (85 g) unsweetened shredded coconut
1 cup (168 g) hemp seeds
¼ cup (85 g) preferred liquid sweetener
¼ cup (30 g) cacao powder
2 tablespoons (15 g) mesquite powder
1 cup (236 ml) almond milk, or as needed
¼ cup (59 ml) melted cacao butter

Cacao nibs, for garnish

TO MAKE THE CRUST: Pulse the hazelnuts into powder in your food processor, then add the cacao and raisins and process until it begins to stick together. Press into the bottom of a parchment paper–lined springform pan and place in the fridge.

TO MAKE THE CAKE: Blend all the ingredients until smooth and combined, using as much almond milk as will get it creamy but keep it thick and adding the cacao butter last. Spread evenly onto your crust and refrigerate overnight. Sprinkle with cacao nibs and indulge, guilt-free!

Peppermint Chocolate Molten Lava Cakes

These are the epitome of raw chocolate decadence. You have a crumbly chocolate cake encasing a lava flow of mint-flavored chocolate sauce; e-p-i-t-o-m-e. I made another version of these for my blog—but without mint, and with the addition of goji berries—and it is still one of my most popular recipes. These are great to share for a romantic night, or whenever you like. Have a tall glass of non-dairy milk nearby!

> Makes: 4 medium or 2 large

CAKE
¹⁄₃ cup (30 g) oats
¹⁄₃ cup (34 g) raw pecans
1 heaping tablespoon (9 g) cacao powder
²⁄₃ cup (116 g) pitted dates, or more as needed

MOLTEN LAVA MIDDLE
¹⁄₃ cup (79 ml) melted cacao butter
¹⁄₃ cup (59 g) pitted dates
2 heaping tablespoons (18 g) cacao powder
¹⁄₈ teaspoon ground cinnamon
¹⁄₈ teaspoon Himalayan sea salt
¹⁄₈ teaspoon chili powder
5-10 drops peppermint oil
Vegan milk

Cacao nibs, for garnish
Fresh mint leaves, for garnish

TO MAKE THE CAKES: Pulse the oats, pecans and cacao powder in your food processor until they become like flour. Add the dates and process until it all starts to stick together. Note: For this recipe you need the mixture to be very sticky, so if you need to, add more dates. Using about two-thirds of the mixture (you have to save some for the tops), press into the bottom and sides of lined cupcake tins and put in the fridge until you need them in the next step. Use the rest of the mixture to make the tops by pressing it into cookie molds the same diameter of your cupcake tins. Put in the fridge until you need them in the last step.

TO MAKE THE MOLTEN MIDDLE: Blend all the ingredients until smooth, adding the milk, as needed, to make it creamy and lavalike (it's a legitimate consistency, okay?). Take the cakes out of the cupcake molds and pour the molten mixture into each one, filling up almost to the top. Now carefully place the tops onto the cakes, gently pressing together the edges. Flip over and decorate with cacao nibs and mint leaves. Let's get molten!

Ginger Lime Berry Ice-Cream Swirl Cheesecake

Fresh, light flavors make this creamy cake something to be desired. It's a cross between a cheesecake and an ice-cream cake because there are layers of a ginger and lime cheesecake swirled together with a simple berry ice cream; for this reason you need to keep it in the freezer. Oh—and the crust is optional, but it adds another texture. Enjoy!

> Makes: 1 cake, 8 to 12 servings

CRUST
¾ cup (68 g) oats
¾ cup (132 g) pitted dates

CHEESECAKE
2 cups (290 g) raw cashews
2 tablespoons (30 ml) melted coconut oil
1 tablespoon (13 g) peeled and chopped fresh ginger
1 cup (175 g) pitted dates
½ cup (118 ml) water, or as needed
2 tablespoons (30 ml) freshly squeezed lime juice

ICE CREAM
2½ cups (510 g) frozen berries

TO MAKE THE CRUST: Process the oats into flour in your food processor, then add the dates and process until everything begins to stick together. Press into the bottom of small cake pan and put in the fridge until you add the next layers.

TO MAKE THE CHEESECAKE AND ICE CREAM: Blend the ingredients for each one separately until smooth. Transfer each mixture to a separate bowl. Spread some berry ice cream evenly over your crust, then some cheesecake mixture; keep alternating as you like until you run out. Put in the freezer overnight, or until solid—then enjoy! It's best when you let it thaw for just a few minutes.

chapter 2

Bites, Bars & Cookies

IN THIS CHAPTER you're going to find all sorts of goodies you can cut up and enjoy in a single bite, or maybe a few. From truffles to cookies to delicious donuts (yep, donuts), and everything in between. These recipes are easy to store, and you can adjust the amount of ingredients according to how much you want. Going to a party? Better double the recipe. Just want to indulge on your own tonight? Halve it and keep the rest for later. Actually I usually eat about half of the recipe components as I am making them but . . . well, shh.

These recipes are great for bringing to picnics or other casual functions, and I mean, who doesn't want a raw fudge brownie to magically appear on their doorstep? (If you didn't catch that, I am saying that they also make great gifts.) Most of them are great for traveling and simply satisfying spontaneous sweet tooth desires. I seriously live at the whim of my taste buds, so whenever a caramel chocolate square is all I can think of, these recipes are my heroes.

As usual in this particular cookbook, the best part is that these recipes are 100 percent guilt-free. I could not give one flying fig about the calorie content and all that other stuff people worry so much over. You just don't need to stress! These are chock-full of whole foods that are excellent for your entire body, inside and out. People tell me my skin has a natural glow to it and they ask why I'm so lucky. I tell them I eat lots of brownies.

Caramel Mocha Bars

If you love rich and sweet treats, this might very well be the best recipe in this whole book.

> Makes: about 9 bars

CRUST
1 cup (145 g) raw almonds
1 cup (175 g) pitted dates

CARAMEL
1/2 cup (130 g) raw cashew butter
1/2 cup (118 ml) coconut oil
1 cup (175 g) pitted dates
Pinch of salt
1/2 teaspoon vanilla extract
1/2 cup (43 g) unsweetened shredded coconut (optional)

MOCHA LAYER
1/3 cup (79 ml) coconut oil
1 to 2 tablespoons (8 to 15 g) cacao powder
1 to 2 tablespoons (8 to 15 g) finely ground coffee beans (optional)
1/4 cup (85 g) preferred liquid sweetener

TO MAKE THE CRUST: Pulse the almonds into flour in your food processor, then add the dates and process until it all begins to stick together. Press into the bottom of a baking pan and refrigerate until you add the next layers.

TO MAKE BOTH THE CARAMEL AND MOCHA LAYERS: Just blend the ingredients in each list until smooth. Spread the caramel onto your crust, followed by the mocha layer. Refrigerate until completely set, preferably overnight. Slice, bite, feel the caffeine!

Cranberry Bliss Bars

Let's create whole-food treats that we can feel proud of eating, for ourselves, our earth and our animal buddies! These healthified (it's a word, okay) bars are chock-full of fiber, protein and healthy fats. They are pretty dense, though, so I'm guessing you'll just need one. I had one for breakfast and it gave me loads of energy for the day. If you want more than that—go for it. Then have a dance party to stay sexy.

> Makes: 8 large bars

BLONDIE CAKE BASE

1 cup (90 g) oats
1 cup (170 g) buckwheat groats
1 cup (175 g) pitted dates
1 teaspoon vanilla extract
1 teaspoon orange zest

SWEET CREAM CHEESE ICING

1 cup (145 g) raw cashews
¼ cup (59 ml) freshly squeezed lemon juice
1 tablespoon (15 ml) melted coconut oil
⅓ cup (115 g) agave nectar

WHITE ORANGE DRIZZLE & CRANBERRIES

3 tablespoons (45 ml) melted cacao butter
3 tablespoons (45 ml) freshly squeezed orange juice
¼ teaspoon stevia (optional, to sweeten and thicken)
¼ cup (30 g) dried cranberries
1 teaspoon orange zest

TO MAKE THE BASE: Pulse the oats and groats (LOL) in your food processor until they become a coarse flour. Add the dates, vanilla and orange zest and process until it forms a ball. Press into the bottom of a parchment paper-lined baking pan. Set aside, or if you want it to be more like baked cake, dehydrate it for a couple of hours in a dehydrator or use your oven at its lowest temperature.

TO MAKE THE CREAM CHEESE ICING: Blend all the ingredients until smooth. It's more flavorful if you let it sit a day or two, but using it right away is fine, too. It's gonna be delicious either way. Spread this over your cake.

TO MAKE THE DRIZZLE: Blend the melted cacao butter and orange juice together. Add the stevia, if you want. Sprinkle the dried cranberries and orange zest onto your cake, then drizzle on the drizzle. Let it set for a few hours in the fridge. Then enjoy!

Creamy Peanut & Oat Squares with Raw Chocolate and Blueberry Topping

These kind of remind me of something you might find at a coffee shop, next to giant muffins and panini. However, they differ in that they only contain high-quality, wholesome ingredients that aren't overloaded with empty calories. Go ahead and cut yourself a big piece and enjoy for your breakfast, snack or dessert. You can up the decadence of this recipe by adding a thin layer of raw chocolate (page 209) over the oats.

> Makes: 12 to 16

OAT LAYER

1 cup (90 g) oats

½ cup (10 g) raw peanut butter

⅓ cup (79 ml) melted coconut oil

⅓ cup (115 g) pure maple syrup

½ cup (43 g) unsweetened shredded coconut

1 teaspoon vanilla extract

1 cup (145 g) fresh or frozen blueberries and/or other fruit you like

MAKE THE OAT LAYER: Mix all the ingredients together until the oats are evenly coated with the wet ingredients. Press into the bottom of a lined 9-inch (23-cm) square pan. Put in the fridge until it's set, about 2 hours. Then layer the blueberries on top and slice.

Ultimate Caramel Chocolate Squares

These are way better than any packaged chocolate bar I've ever had, not only because they really do taste better but also since they are made with only wholesome ingredients and love! This is another great recipe to share with those who doubt that "healthy" and "indulgent" can be included in the same dish—chocolate always wins 'em over.

> Makes: about 12

BASE
2 cups (290 g) raw almonds
1½ cups (263 g) pitted dates
Splash of vanilla extract

CARAMEL LAYER
1 cup (175 g) pitted dates
1 tablespoon (15 ml) melted coconut oil
¼ cup water
Splash of vanilla extract
Pinch of sea salt

CHOCOLATE LAYER
2 tablespoons (30 ml) melted coconut oil
¼ cup (30 g) cacao powder
2½ tablespoons (50 g) pure maple syrup
¼ teaspoon chili powder

TO MAKE THE BASE LAYER: Pulse the almonds into flour, then add dates and vanilla and process until it begins to stick together. Press into the bottom of a parchment paper-lined 9-inch (23-cm) square baking pan and place in the fridge until you add the caramel layer.

TO MAKE THE CARAMEL AND CHOCOLATE LAYERS: Blend all the caramel ingredients until smooth, and then spread onto the crust. Then do this for the chocolate layer, too, and spread it over the caramel layer. Let it sit in the fridge overnight and then slice and serve the next day. So good.

Orange Carob Bars & Almond Chocolate Bars

These are both easy and quick to make, and a welcome gift to any party. People get excited when they see fancy chocolate, and just imagine their faces when you tell them it's healthy and homemade—you're going to make some new friends. Even if you don't bring this to a party, it's a great treat to enjoy by yourself after dinner. I recommend drinking white wine with the orange carob bars, and red with the almond chocolate bars.

> Makes: about 4 servings

ORANGE CAROB BARS

1/3 cup (35 g) carob powder
1/4 cup (59 ml) melted coconut oil
2 1/2 tablespoons (50 g) pure maple syrup
1/2 teaspoon vanilla extract
Juice and zest of 1 orange

ALMOND CHOCOLATE BARS

1/3 cup (40 g) cacao powder
1/3 cup (79 ml) melted coconut oil
2 1/2 tablespoons (50 g) pure maple syrup
1/2 teaspoon almond oil
1/4 cup (37 g) roughly chopped raw almonds

MAKE THE ORANGE CAROB BARS: Mix all the ingredients together until smooth. Spread thinly onto the bottom of a small parchment paper–lined baking pan and put in the fridge until it has hardened, about 1 hour. Cut into bars, then enjoy!

MAKE THE ALMOND CHOCOLATE BARS: Follow the same instructions as above, but leave out the chopped almonds until the end, and gently sprinkle them on top before you put the chocolate in the fridge.

Loco Coco Bars

I named these Loco Coco Bars because they contain coconut, cacao and are crazy—loco—good. If you don't like the taste of raisins (they are slightly tarter), go ahead and use dates instead. These can be paired with a tall glass of cold vegan milk for a mouthwatering afternoon treat.

> Makes: 10 to 12

BASE

1 cup (90 g) oats

1 cup (100 g) raw walnuts

2 cups (290 g) raisins

2 tablespoons (15 g) cacao powder

COCONUT TOPPING

2 tablespoons (30 ml) melted coconut oil

2 tablespoons (11 g) unsweetened shredded coconut

1 teaspoon raw sugar or date paste (page 210)

CHOCOLATE TOPPING

2 tablespoons (15 g) cacao powder

2 tablespoons (30 ml) melted coconut oil

2 tablespoons (31 g) raw sugar or date paste (page 210)

TO MAKE THE BASE: Pulse the oats and walnuts in your food processor until they become a coarse flour. Add the raisins and cacao and process until it all sticks together. Press into the bottom of a lined 9-inch (23-cm) square pan and put in the fridge until you add the toppings.

TO MAKE THE TOPPINGS: Mix the ingredients for each in separate bowls, until smooth. Pour onto the base layer and sprinkle with extra coconut, if desired. Let it set in the fridge for 30 minutes, cut into bars, then dig in.

Superfood Brownies with Chile Cinnamon Fudge Frosting

Brownies definitely play a large role in the net happiness of the world. They can turn a dull day into a bright one, and a frown into a smile. With raw vegan brownies, it's also very rewarding knowing that the special chocolate treat in your hand didn't require any harm to others, and it's good for your body! The hemp seeds, walnuts and flax are great for your hair, skin, nails and brain functioning. The chile and cinnamon in the frosting boost your metabolism and help with detoxification, and the cacao powder is full of fiber. Celebrate good times—c'mon!

> Makes: 9 large brownies

BROWNIES
1 cup (100 g) raw walnuts
4 cups (672 g) flaxseeds
½ cup (84 g) hemp seeds
1 cup (175 g) pitted dates
1 cup (145 g) raisins
2 tablespoons (15 g) cacao powder
1 teaspoon vanilla extract
Pinch of salt (optional)

FROSTING
1 avocado, peeled and pitted
1 to 2 tablespoons (8 to 15 g) cacao powder
2 tablespoons (40 g) pure maple syrup
¼ teaspoon ground cinnamon
¼ teaspoon chili powder
1 tablespoon (15 ml) melted coconut oil

TO MAKE THE BROWNIES: Pulse the walnuts and flaxseeds in your food processor until they become a coarse flour, add the rest of the ingredients and process until it all starts to stick together. Press evenly into the bottom of a parchment paper-lined 9-inch (23-cm) square baking pan and put in the fridge for about an hour.

TO MAKE THE FROSTING: Blend all the ingredients until smooth and thick. Put in the fridge to thicken it up more, if needed. When your brownies are set, frost them, slice and enjoy.

Chocolate Energy Bites with Pumpkin Seeds, Raisins & Maca

These are great for traveling snacks and to just get through those tough days! Make them with kids, if you don't mind a bit of a chocolate mess.

> Makes: about 10

CHOCOLATE
¼ cup (59 ml) melted cacao butter
¼ cup (30 g) cacao powder
1 tablespoon (8 g) maca powder
2 tablespoons (40 g) preferred liquid sweetener

TOPPINGS
Raisins
Raw pumpkin seeds
Raw walnuts
Goji berries

TO MAKE THE CHOCOLATE: Mix all the ingredients together until smooth. Pour into circles and press on your toppings. Put them in the fridge for 1 to 2 hours, or until solid.

Almond Joys with Crunchy Coconut Center Enrobed in Raw Chocolate

These are a little bit addictive for coconut lovers. My mom does not have a very big sweet tooth but she devoured these in minutes, because she loved Almond Joys while growing up. I see that as a job well done on my part! The best compliment is when someone can't stop eating your recipe, or asks for seconds.

> Makes: 6 large

CHOCOLATE
4 tablespoons (60 ml) melted cacao butter
1/4 cup (30 g) cacao powder
2 tablespoon (40 g) preferred liquid sweetener

COCONUT CENTERS
1 1/4 cups (107 g) unsweetened shredded coconut
1 tablespoon (15 ml) melted coconut oil, or as needed
1 tablespoon (20 g) agave nectar, or as needed

TO MAKE THE CHOCOLATE: Mix all the ingredients together until smooth. Set aside.

TO MAKE THE COCONUT CENTERS: Put half of the coconut into your food processor and process until you get a chunky butter consistency; it may take several minutes. Add the rest of the ingredients, including the remaining coconut, and process until it all sticks together. If it's too dry, add more coconut oil or agave nectar. Press this mixture into flattened balls and put in the fridge for an hour, until they set. Then dip in the chocolate and allow the chocolate to set. Finally—eat.

Piña Colada Bites with Pineapple, Coconut & Pine Nuts

Here is a quick recipe that you can whip up for a sweet snack any day. The combination of pineapple and coconut is one that's tried and true—and I think the addition of pine nuts here only improves on that by adding another layer of flavor.

> Makes: about 20

½ cup (70 g) raw pine nuts

½ cup (75 g) dried pineapple

½ cup (43 g) unsweetened shredded coconut

1 tablespoon (15 ml) melted coconut oil, or as needed

¼ cup (28 g) goji berries

Pulse the pine nuts into flour in your food processor, then add the rest of the ingredients and process until it all starts to stick together. If it's too dry, add some coconut oil. Adjust the mixture according to taste, then roll into balls and let them set in the fridge for a few hours—or gobble them down immediately.

Fruit Crumble with Banana Ice Cream

This is perfect for summer. In fact, I just enjoyed a bowl of it in my backyard in the well-seasoned sunshine. If you'd rather have a smoothie to cool down—blend all the ingredients until smooth, adding some ice, and you've got one tall glass of deliciousness.

> Makes: 3 to 4 servings

CRUMBLE
½ cup (50 g) raw walnuts
½ cup (45 g) rolled oats
½ cup (88 g) pitted dates
Ground cinnamon

FRUIT
2 peaches, pitted
1 pear, cored
½ cup (75 g) blueberries
Whatever other fruit you like!
3 bananas, frozen

Pulse the ingredients in your food processor until it gets a granola-like consistency, pulsing in cinnamon to taste. Transfer to a bowl. Chop your fruit and mix into the crumble. Blend the bananas until smooth and creamy and scoop onto your fruit crumble. Yum.

Crazy for Coconut Bars

These are bliss for those who love the smell, flavor and essence of coconut. I am one of said people, so I could hardly stop eating the mixture before I put it in the fridge. As a bonus, you can rub leftovers on your skin for a hydrating scrub! These are a perfect pre- or postworkout snack because coconut gives you long-lasting energy and helps slowly release the carbs in the sweetener. Coconut is a superfood! Get it in ya!

> Makes: 4 bars

2 cups (170 g) unsweetened shredded coconut

1 heaping tablespoon (20 ml) coconut oil

2 to 4 tablespoons (40 to 85 g) preferred liquid sweetener

Put 1 cup (85 g) of the coconut into your food processor and blend until the oil begins to come out and the coconut becomes more like a chunky butter; this may take several minutes. Add the rest of the ingredients and process until fully combined. Press into the bottom of a parchment paper-lined pan and put in the fridge for an hour, or until set. Slice and enjoy! These can be stored for up to a week in the fridge.

Superior Fudge

Why is it superior? Because it's good for you, doesn't hurt anybody and tastes even better than the original version. Nuff said.

> Makes: 8 pieces

1 cup (175 g) pitted dates
¼ cup (64 g) raw cashew butter
½ cup (55 g) coconut butter
2 tablespoons (15 g) cacao powder
½ teaspoon vanilla powder

Put everything into your food processor and blend until very smooth and sticky. Press into the bottom of a baking pan and refrigerate for an hour or two, until set. Slice and indulge in peace.

Maca Cacao Truffles

These can be whipped up in minutes and are terrific for traveling or providing lots of energy for busy days, tough workouts or life in general. Maca helps balance hormones and has been known to enhance libido . . . oh baby!

> Makes: about 10 truffles

½ cup (50 g) raw walnuts

½ cup (84 g) hemp seeds

1 cup (175 g) pitted dates

2 tablespoons (15 g) maca powder, plus more for coating, if desired

1 teaspoon cacao powder, plus more for coating, if desired

½ teaspoon vanilla powder (optional)

Put the walnuts and hemp seeds into your food processor and process until they turn into powder. Add the rest of the ingredients and process until it all sticks together. Roll the mixture into balls and then coat in maca or cacao powder if desired. Yahoo!

Spiced Orange Chocolate Layered with Fresh Kiwi, Orange & Dried Figs

The combination of orange and chocolate is pure genius! If you've never tried it, you're in for a treat.

> Makes: 3 servings

RAW ORANGE CHOCOLATE
3 tablespoons (45 ml) melted coconut oil

1 to 2 tablespoons (20 to 40 g) agave or pure maple syrup

2 tablespoons (15 g) cacao powder

1/4 teaspoon vanilla extract

1/4 teaspoon ground cinnamon

Zest of 1 orange

Pinch of salt

FRUIT LAYERS
1 kiwi

1 orange

4 figs

GOJI BERRY COULIS
1/4 cup (28 g) dried goji berries barely covered in water

1 tablespoon (20 g) agave nectar

Other berries (optional)

TO MAKE THE CHOCOLATE: Stir all ingredients together by hand until smooth and *so yummy*. On parchment paper, take a spoonful of the chocolate and spread it into a circle about 2 inches (5 cm) in diameter. Do this until you run out; you should end up with six or so. Put in the freezer.

TO MAKE THE FRUIT LAYERS: Slice all the fruit.

TO MAKE THE BERRY COULIS: Blend the goji berries with their water and the agave until smooth. If you have other berries, add those, if you like.

NOW PUT IT ALL TOGETHER: Take the chocolate out of the freezer; it should now be solid. Decorate plates with the coulis as you desire, then layer on the chocolate disks and fruit slices.

Chocolate Banana Crêpes with Coconut Cream & Berries

Gettin' fancy with it here. Make sure to keep a close eye on your crêpes—the first time I tried making these, they dehydrated for too long and weren't pliable enough. Otherwise, these would make a wonderful surprise breakfast for someone special if ya know what I'm sayin'...ehhh?

> Makes: 3 crêpes

CRÊPES
3 bananas
1 tablespoon (8 g) cacao powder
⅓ cup (59 g) pitted dates

FILLINGS
Coconut cream (page 207)
Fresh berries and other fruit

Blend all the crêpe ingredients until smooth. Spread into crêpe shapes on dehydrator trays and dehydrate for about 12 hours, or until they have dried but are still flexible—kind of like a tortilla. Fill these with the coconut cream and fruit, roll up and eat!

Chocolate Nut Butter Cups, Three Ways

These are the epitome of sweet decadence. You cannot achieve greater perfection than creamy nut butter wrapped with raw dark chocolate, sprinkled with cacao nibs and sea salt. I chose to use three different kinds of nut butter because, simply put, on countless occasions, variety is the spice of life. You can use whatever kind you want—I decided on sesame seed butter, almond butter and jungle peanut butter. These are also used in my rawified Reese's cake (page 20), in mini form.

> Makes: 10 to 12

CHOCOLATE CUPS
1/3 cup (79 ml) melted coconut oil
2 1/2 tablespoons (50 g) pure maple syrup
1/3 cup (40 g) cacao powder
1 teaspoon vanilla extract

FILLINGS
About 3 tablespoons (45 g) sesame seed butter (tahini)
About 3 tablespoons (48 g) raw peanut butter
About 3 tablespoons (48 g) raw almond butter

Sea salt, for garnish
Cacao nibs, for garnish

Mix together the ingredients in a bowl until smooth. Get about a dozen cupcake papers (use smaller liners for mini butter cups) and brush the inside with the chocolate mixture so the bottoms and sides are evenly coated with chocolate. (If it is too runny and doesn't stick, let it chill and thicken for about 10 minutes.) Put these in the fridge for 30 minutes, or until hardened. Fill each with about 1 teaspoon of one of the nut butters, and then pour the remaining chocolate on top. (You may have to melt the chocolate again so it can be poured.) Put back in the fridge for 20 minutes, or until hardened. Sprinkle with sea salt and cacao nibs and serve with nut milk. Mmm . . . there is no better treat.

Avocado Towers with Dark Chocolate Mousse & Cinnamon Pistachios

This recipe is very simple and impressive to look at, so it makes a perfect dessert after a romantic dinner with your beau. Or maybe you just deserve a special treat for yourself! You are awesome, so I think you should go for it. Anyway—it tastes even better than it looks. And peeling an avocado is actually quite fun, or maybe I am just too easily entertained.

> Makes: 1 tower, 1 to 2 servings

CHOCOLATE LAYER
1 banana
1 heaping tablespoon (9 g) cacao powder
1 tablespoon (20 g) pure maple syrup
1 tablespoon (15 ml) melted coconut oil
1/4 teaspoon vanilla extract

COATINGS
1/4 teaspoon cinnamon
1 tablespoon (7 g) roughly chopped raw pecans
1 tablespoon (9 g) roughly chopped raw pistachios

AVOCADO LAYER
1 avocado

TO MAKE THE CHOCOLATE LAYER: Blend all the ingredients until smooth and put in the fridge until it thickens, about 30 minutes.

TO COAT THE NUTS: Mix the nuts with the cinnamon in a bowl until coated.

ASSEMBLY: Peel the avocado carefully and then cut horizontally into thick slices, gently removing the pit when you get to it. Make sure you keep the order of the slices. Now layer them, spreading a bit of the chocolate mixture on top of each piece as you go, until you use everything up. Gently press the chopped nuts onto the outside of the tower and eat right away! Mmm . . . avocado in my belly.

Go-Nuts Donuts with Frosting & Fruit Sprinkles

These are way too cute to eat, but they were promptly devoured anyway. I love decorating them and carefully sprinkling on the toppings. These would be terrific for a do-it-yourself dessert party! Dehydrating the donuts is optional, but it helps them hold together better. There are endless possibilities with the combinations here, so I expect you will get creative. You can also add cacao, vanilla, maca or anything else to the donut mixture to change the flavor of donuts. Donut party: initiate!

> Makes: 3 large donuts or 6 mini donuts

DONUTS
2 cups (290 g) raw almonds
2¼ cups (327 g) golden raisins

CHOCOLATE FROSTING
1 tablespoon (8 g) cacao powder
1 tablespoon (15 ml) melted coconut oil
1 tablespoon (20 g) pure maple syrup

STRAWBERRY FROSTING
1 tablespoon (15 ml) melted coconut oil
2 large strawberries, hulled and sliced

COCONUT FROSTING
1 tablespoon (15 ml) melted coconut oil
1 tablespoon (6 g) unsweetened shredded coconut
1 tablespoon (20 g) pure maple syrup

SPRINKLES
1 tablespoon (9 g) diced dried papaya
1 tablespoon (99 g) diced golden raisins
1 tablespoon (7 g) diced goji berries
1 tablespoon (5 g) raw coconut flakes
1 tablespoon (8 g) cacao nibs

TO MAKE THE DONUTS: Pulse the almonds in your food processor until they become a coarse flour. Add the raisins and process until it begins to stick together. Press into donut molds and dehydrate for 2 hours, or use your oven at its lowest temperature, then stick in the fridge for 30 minutes. You could also just put them right in the fridge without dehydrating.

TO MAKE THE FROSTINGS: For each, simply mix the ingredients together until smooth, and then drizzle over your donuts. Next are the sprinkles! Then into your mouth. Donut party: complete.

Avocado Mint Cream Bars with Chocolate, Two Ways

These are surprisingly delicious. When I first made them, I was, of course, expecting them to taste good, but I was seriously excited when I took my first bite of the finished product. They are creamy, sweet, minty and chocolaty all at once. I was originally going to call them Nanaimo bars but after tasting them, I felt they deserved a name unto themselves. Think of mint chocolate chip ice cream, in square form — that's what these are. Note: You can either use a banana in the filling and freeze the recipe to make ice-cream sandwich bars (smart move) or use coconut meat and keep in the fridge (also an intelligent choice). No wrong moves here, folks.

> Makes: about 14

BASE
1 cup (145 g) raw almonds
1 cup (175 g) raw pitted dates
1 heaping tablespoon (9 g) cacao powder

MIDDLE
1 avocado, peeled and pitted
3 tablespoons (45 ml) melted coconut oil
3 to 4 (60 to 85 g) tablespoons pure maple syrup
1 banana, or 1 cup (80 g) fresh young coconut meat
½ teaspoon vanilla extract
Pinch of salt (optional)
5-10 drops peppermint oil

TOP
3 tablespoons (23 g) cacao powder
3 tablespoons (45 ml) melted coconut oil
2 tablespoons (40 g) pure maple syrup

TO MAKE THE BASE: Pulse all the ingredients in your food processor until they stick together. Press evenly into the bottom of a lined 9-inch (23-cm) square baking pan. Put in the fridge while you make the next layer.

TO MAKE THE MIDDLE: Blend all in the ingredients until smooth and thick, then spread over your base layer and put back in the fridge.

TO MAKE THE TOP: Mix all the ingredients together until smooth, pour evenly on top of your middle layer and put in the fridge or freezer, depending on what ingredient you used in the middle.

Endless Energy Bars with Nuts, Seeds, Figs, Raisins & Sweet Coconut Drizzle

These energy bars will keep you going strong all day; whether you've just finished a workout, are about to begin a tough hike, or just need some whole-food goodness to get through your busy day—they've got you covered. Absolutely full of superfoods, such as chia seeds, goji berries, almonds, cacao nibs and coconut oil, they taste like heaven and will you make feel like you're flying.

> Makes: about 10

BARS
¼ cup (25 g) raw pecans
¼ cup (37 g) raw almonds
2 tablespoons (21 g) chia seeds
2 tablespoons (24 g) hemp seeds
2 tablespoons (17 g) raw pumpkin seeds
2 tablespoons (19 g) sunflower seeds
2 tablespoons (16 g) cacao nibs
1 cup (145 g) raisins
⅓ cup (59 g) dried figs
Pinch of salt (optional)

COCONUT DRIZZLE
2 tablespoons (30 ml) melted coconut oil
1 tablespoon (20 g) preferred liquid sweetener

TO MAKE THE BARS: Put all the ingredients into your food processor and process until everything begins to stick together. Press into the bottom of a lined 9-inch (23-cm) square baking pan and put in the fridge for 2 to 3 hours, until set.

TO MAKE THE DRIZZLE: Mix the ingredients until combined. Get your pan out of the fridge and take out the square of energy bars. Cut into individual bars and then drizzle each with the coconut mixture. Let the coconut oil resolidify—then chow down! These can be stored in the fridge or freezer for about 1 week.

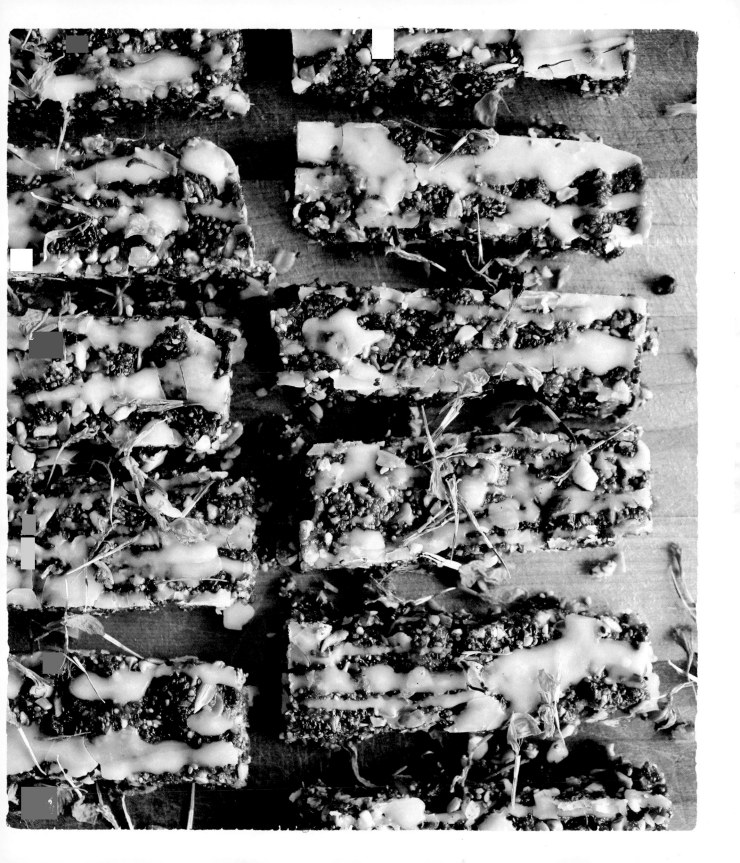

Totally Tahini Cups with Coffee Cream Filling

Simple, sublime, stylish . . . sassy? Okay, enough with the alliteration. These are just plain yummy. I know not everyone has a major sweet tooth like me, so this recipe is for those folks. Tahini is delicious, but it is also quite bitter. It has a strong nutty flavor (from the sesame seeds it's made of) that goes perfectly with savory meals. However—its nutty bitterness can still work wonderfully in desserts as well. Here, it's combined with salt and coconut oil to make a shell encompassing sweet coffee-date cream. Can you say *yum!*? Probably not, because your mouth will be too full of these terrifically tasty tahini cups . . . Duh. Did it again.

> Makes: 6 cups

TAHINI SHELL
⅓ cup (80 g) tahini
⅓ cup (79 ml) melted coconut oil

COFFEE CREAM
1 cup (175 g) pitted dates
½ cup (118 ml) strong brewed coffee, or as needed

Salt

TO MAKE THE SHELL: Combine the ingredients by hand or in a food processor until smooth. It will be a bit watery but the coconut oil will harden up in the fridge. Pour half of the mixture into the bottom of 6 cupcake liners and put in the fridge for 20 minutes, or until solid. Set aside the other half of the tahini mixture.

TO MAKE THE FILLING: Put all the ingredients into your food processor and process until smooth and very thick, adding the coffee, as needed. This could take a few minutes, and you may have to stop the food processor to wipe down the sides a few times so everything continues to combine evenly.

ASSEMBLY: Scoop a dollop of the filling into each of the hardened bottoms in your cupcake papers. Pour enough of the remaining tahini mixture on each to cover the dollop. Put back in the fridge for about 20 minutes, or until solid, then sprinkle with salt and enjoy!

Fudge Bites

Gooey Medjool dates filled with various nut butters, covered in raw chocolate and dipped in sesame seeds, coconut and chopped nuts . . . can it get any more decadent yet simple? I don't think so. I used tahini, almond butter and peanut butter for the fillings and each one had its own special flavor. Like the name says, these taste a bit like chocolate nut fudge, thanks to the sweet chewiness of the dates. Mmm . . . dates . . .

> Makes: 3

3 large Medjool dates, pitted

$\frac{1}{2}$ teaspoon each of your three favorite raw nut butters

2 to 3 tablespoons (30 to 45 ml) liquid raw chocolate (page 209)

Sesame seeds, to coat

Unsweetened shredded coconut, to coat

Chopped nuts, to coat

Fill the dates with the nut butter. Dip in the chocolate, then roll in the coatings. Let the chocolate harden for 30 minutes in the fridge—then enjoy!

Hippie Halva

You can add other ingredients to this recipe—for example, coconut oil, cacao, pistachios or maple syrup—but I decided to keep it simple here as a basic halva recipe. With just two ingredients, the warm creaminess of the sesame seeds is at the front followed by the subtle sweetness of the dates. Salt is optional but it does wonders in bringing out the flavors. Have fun!

> Makes: 4 to 6 servings

1 cup (144 g) raw hulled sesame seeds
½ cup (175 g) pitted dates
Salt
Finely ground dried coconut, for coating

Process the sesame seeds into sesame seed butter (a.k.a. tahini) in your food processor. It will take several minutes and you may have to stop a few times, but be patient! It'll eventually turn into a thick butter—trust me. Add the dates (and salt to taste, if using) and process until it is a thick, smooth mixture. Press into a small loaf pan and refrigerate for a few hours, until set. Cut into squares, roll in ground coconut for a powdered sugar coating effect and eat!

Pecan Sesame Truffles with Camu Camu, Orange & Vanilla

This recipe has a lot of things going on, but they all work wonderfully together. I actually was planning on making simple orange truffles when I started up my food processor but spontaneity had another idea. I ended up adding a bunch of different ingredients and it turned out great! Roll your finished truffles in a variety of powders for contrast.

> Makes: 6 very large truffles

1 cup (100 g) raw pecans

Juice of 1 orange

2 teaspoons camu camu powder, plus more as needed

1 teaspoon vanilla powder, plus more as needed

1 cup (145 g) raisins

½ cup (72 g) sesame seeds

½ cup (43 g) unsweetened shredded coconut

Ground cinnamon (optional)

In your food processor, pulse the pecans into flour. Add all the other ingredients—except the sesame seeds, coconut and cinnamon—and process until it all begins to form a wet ball. Add the sesame seeds. If the mixture is still too wet, add other powders or flours. Roll into balls, using your hands or an ice-cream scoop. Coat in whatever you like; I used camu camu powder, vanilla powder, sesame seeds, dried coconut and cinnamon.

Almond Butter and Jelly Sandwiches with Apple Bread

Almond butter jelly time! It doesn't get more comfort foody than this. The apple bread is quite a treat, and it goes perfectly with the creamy nut butter and the sweet, fresh jam. Kids will love this one for breakfast or a snack, especially served with cold almond milk! You can use peanut butter, if you like, to get the ultimate experience of the much-loved original.

> Makes: about 4 sandwiches

APPLE BREAD
1 cup (145 g) raw almonds
1 cup (175 g) pitted dates
1 apple, peeled and cored

JAM
1 cup (145 g) berries
3 pitted dates
1 tablespoon (10 g) chia seeds
Freshly squeezed lemon juice, water, or liquid sweetener (optional)

Raw almond butter, raw peanut butter, or other favorite raw nut butter
Bananas, sliced

TO MAKE THE APPLE BREAD: Pulse the almonds into flour in your food processor, and then add the dates and apple and process until it begins to stick together and forms a ball. Spread evenly onto dehydrator sheets and dehydrate for 4 to 6 hours, until the bread is pliable and you can slice it. Alternatively, you can put it in the oven at its lowest temperature.

TO MAKE THE JAM: Blend up the berries and dates, and then add the chia seeds so it all gels together. If it's too watery, add more chia seeds. If it's too thick, add some lemon juice, water or liquid sweetener.

Spread the jam and almond butter onto your sliced apple bread. Top with bananas! Love it!

Maca Miracle Pyramids with Chocolate Goji Berry Filling

These are delicious and great for giving you energy for the whole day. Maca and cacao are excellent for your brain, balancing hormones and circulation.

> Makes: 3 pyramids

MACA TRIANGLES

2 tablespoons (40 g) pure maple syrup
2 tablespoons (15 g) maca powder
2 tablespoons (30 ml) coconut oil

CHOCOLATE FILLING

2 tablespoons (15 g) cacao powder
2 tablespoons (38 g) cacao butter
2 tablespoons (40 g) preferred liquid sweetener
¼ cup (28 g) goji berries

TO MAKE THE TRIANGLES: Mix together the ingredients until smooth. Spread evenly on parchment paper and refrigerate until solid. Use triangular cookie cutters to cut into triangles, and then put back in the fridge.

TO MAKE THE FILLING: Mix together all the ingredients—except the goji berries—until smooth. Throw in the goji berries. Now carefully connect the sides of your triangles so you form a pyramid shape, but don't add the bottom yet. Fill with your chocolate mixture, then add the final triangle to make a pyramid. Let them set in the fridge or eat right away!

Raw Chocolate Cookies Sandwiching Vanilla Cashew Cream

These are splendid. I love re-creating popular sweets because many people can identify with them and get excited about a healthy version of their favorite treats. I mean, really—who doesn't love Oreos? I just don't love their long list of processed ingredients. So, here's a simplified Oreo recipe, full of good-for-you stuff, such as oats, cashews, dates and cacao. Relive childhood fun and dip a couple in a glass of vegan milk.

> Makes: about 10

COOKIES
¾ cup (68 g) oats
1 cup (175 g) pitted dates
2 tablespoons (15 g) cacao powder

VANILLA FILLING
½ cup (73 g) raw cashews
2½ tablespoons (50 g) pure maple syrup
2 tablespoons (30 ml) melted coconut oil
1 teaspoon vanilla extract

TO MAKE THE COOKIES: Pulse the oats in your food processor until they become a coarse flour. Add the dates and cacao and process until it forms a semi-sticky dough. If it's too dry, add more dates. Roll the dough as thinly as possible onto parchment paper, then cut cookie shapes with a cookie cutter until you use up all the dough. Optional: Dehydrate for a few hours, or until they harden—this will make them crunch like the original.

TO MAKE THE FILLING: Blend all the ingredients until smooth; you may have to add some water to make it creamy. Put the filling in the fridge for 3 to 4 hours, until thickened.

ASSEMBLY: Spread the vanilla filling evenly onto half of your cookies, then press the remaining cookies on top of the frosted ones.

Peppermint Cream Sandwich Cookies Covered in Chocolate

These are a favorite recipe of mine. I think/hope they will become one of your top picks, too. You have three different textures and flavors going on at the same time and the consequence of this is pure bliss. Man, I keep rhymin' without tryin'.

> Makes: about 9 cookies

COOKIE
1 cup (100 g) raw pecans
3/4 cup (132 g) pitted dates
1 tablespoon (15 ml) melted coconut oil

PEPPERMINT CREAM
1/4 cup (59 ml) coconut oil
Peppermint oil

CHOCOLATE
3 tablespoons (23 g) cacao powder
3 tablespoons (45 ml) melted cacao butter
1 tablespoon (20 g) pure maple syrup

TO MAKE THE COOKIES: Pulse the pecans into flour in your food processor, then add the dates and melted coconut oil and continue to process until they begin to stick together. Press the rough dough into a large ball, then roll it out on parchment paper about 1/4 cm thick. Cut out cookies and put them in the fridge for 2 hours, or until they set.

TO MAKE THE PEPPERMINT CREAM: Put the coconut oil and peppermint oil to taste into your food processor and continually process until the coconut oil is smooth and the peppermint oil is fully incorporated. Spoon small dollops of this onto half of your cookies, then cover them with the remaining cookies. Refrigerate overnight.

TO MAKE THE CHOCOLATE: Mix the ingredients until smooth. Dip your cookies halfway in, then put on parchment paper and into the fridge so they solidify quickly. A few minutes later, they're ready to eat.

Peanut Butter Cookies

Who didn't love peanut butter cookies while growing up? They are a favorite of mine due to my love of peanut butter, and so I figured I'd better create a raw version to satisfy my childhood treat-based cravings. This recipe hits the spot! You can use whatever nut butter you like; cashew butter is delicious, for example. The salt sprinkled on top is optional but adds another texture and enhances the flavor. Eat these the day after you make them—they taste better!

> Makes: 9 to 12 cookies

1 cup (145 g) raw almonds
1/3 cup (87 g) raw peanut butter
1 cup (175 g) pitted Medjool dates
1/2 teaspoon vanilla extract
Salt, for sprinkling

Pulse the almonds into flour in your food processor. Add the rest of the ingredients—except the salt—and process until a crumbly dough forms. Form the dough into balls and gently press them down. Indent with a fork to get the classic look, and then sprinkle lightly with salt. Leave in the fridge overnight.

Carob Comfort Cookies

Exactly as the name implies, these cookies will provide you with comfort and happiness—without the guilt! I think they taste a bit like those "digestive biscuits" everyone loves. When you dehydrate your cookies, it makes them chewy just like the baked version. Experiment with different nuts, or try out oats instead of buckwheat. Many adaptations are possible here; you could add ground cinnamon or ginger to the dough, or different ingredients to the frosting. Delicious possibilities abound!

> Makes: 4 large cookies

COOKIES
½ cup (85 g) buckwheat groats
½ cup (50 g) raw pecans
1 cup (175 g) pitted dates

CAROB FROSTING
3 tablespoons (45 ml) melted coconut oil
3 tablespoons (23 g) carob powder
3 tablespoons (60 g) preferred liquid sweetener

Finely raw chopped nuts, for sprinkling

TO MAKE THE COOKIES: Pulse the buckwheat groats and pecans into flour, then add the dates and process until it all sticks together. Roll out this dough and cut out cookie shapes. Dehydrate for 5 hours, or until they are slightly chewy. You can leave them as is without dehydrating but it gives them the texture of a baked cookie. He-he.

TO MAKE THE FROSTING: Stir together the ingredients and then spread on top of your cookies, followed by finely chopped nuts. Nom!

Rawdical Raisin Cacao Cookies with Oats

Do you miss oatmeal raisin cookies? These are for you. They're made with an oat and maca base, which creates a hearty, caramel-type foundation, sweetened with whatever you like and made complete with cacao nibs and raisins. You can dehydrate them, if you desire, to get the real cookie texture and make them warm! Otherwise, eat them right away for a nutritious, sweet love bite. Yes, a love bite is a thing.

> Makes: 7 very large cookies

¾ cup (68 g) oats
3 tablespoons (60 g) preferred liquid sweetener
3 tablespoons (45 ml) melted coconut oil
2 tablespoons (15 g) maca powder
2 tablespoons (15 g) cacao nibs
¼ cup (35 g) raisins

Process the oats into flour in your food processor. Add the sweetener, coconut oil and maca and pulse until it all sticks together. Mix in the cacao nibs and raisins by hand, then squish into balls, or use an ice-cream scoop. Let them set in the fridge for 3 hours, eat them right away, or dehydrate for 4 to 5 hours so they hold together and get warm.

chapter 3

Pies
& Tarts

"OH ME OH MY, I JUST WANT PIE . . ." I made that up all by myself on the spot, so I'm feelin' pretty good right now.

Next to cake, pies and tarts are my favorite kind of dessert to make, for many of the same reasons. Pie makes people smile. It brings them together to enjoy something sweet, healthy and delicious, and it gives them something to gawk at and talk about. I love seeing the look on peoples' faces when I put a sinful-looking pie down on the table and then tell them that it's super healthy.

I really enjoy the process of making pies and tarts: you whirl together a simple crust in the food processor, then carefully press it into the pie or tart dish, blend together some different layers and evenly spread them into the crust, refrigerate for a little bit, then sprinkle on whatever garnishes are complementary. It's such a gentle, easy set of steps but in the end you wind up with this gorgeous, goodness-filled dessert that everyone is drawn toward. I suppose that's partly because—as with all my recipes—I make an effort to put love into the food I create, and people can sense that. But also they just see a maple pecan pie and can't help but come running.

The tart pans I use vary, so any kind you have will work (the result might just be a different shape, that's all). Try to have these recipes eaten within about five days, because they don't store that well and many of them contain uncovered fresh fruit. I don't think you'll have a problem with this, though . . . wink wink, nudge nudge.

Jungle Pie with Chocolate Crust, Banana Slices & Chunky Coconut Topping

Its cacao apart, I imagine monkeys would love this pie; they dig bananas and coconuts and so do I. That rhyme wasn't intentional; I can't lie. Okay, I'll stop now. This recipe is practically overflowing with super-healthy fats, energy-giving nutrients, big flavor and unrefined love. Drizzle it with some chocolate sauce to complete the bliss experience! Rub it on your face for a moisturizing scrub! Or just eat.

> Makes: 1 pie, 8 to 10 servings

CRUST
1 cup (133 g) raw Brazil nuts
1 tablespoon (8 g) cacao powder
1 cup (175 g) pitted dates

BANANA LAYER
2 to 3 bananas

COCONUT LAYER
3 cups (255 g) unsweetened shredded coconut
$1/4$ cup (85 g) agave nectar
$1/4$ cup (59 ml) melted coconut oil

CHOCOLATE SAUCE
Liquid raw chocolate (page 209)

TO MAKE THE CRUST: Pulse the nuts into powder in your food processor. Add the cacao and dates and process until it all begins to stick together. Press into a tart or pie pan and refrigerate.

TO MAKE THE COCONUT LAYER: Process 2 cups of the coconut into a coconut butter–like consistency. It will take several minutes and doesn't have to be totally smooth. Add the rest of the ingredients and process until it all combines.

Slice your bananas and arrange them in the bottom of your crust; scoop on your coconut mixture and pat down, sealing in the bananas. Refrigerate for an hour or two until set. Then drizzle on the chocolate and go bananas.

Jewel Fruit Tart with Caramel Almond Filling

I love how frozen berries look just like gems, and that is showcased in this recipe. Here's a challenge: try not to eat all of the almond caramel before putting it in your crust.

> Makes: 1 tart, 8 servings

CRUST
2 cups (200 g) raw walnuts
2 cups (290 g) raisins

ALMOND CARAMEL
1/4 cup (64 g) raw almond butter
1/4 cup (59 ml) melted coconut oil
1/4 cup (85 g) pure maple syrup
1/2 teaspoon ground cinnamon
Water

TOPPINGS
3 cups (765 g) frozen berries
(or however much you want)
1/2 cup (56 g) goji berries

TO MAKE THE CRUST: Pulse the walnuts in your food processor until they become a coarse flour. Add the raisins and process until it sticks together, forming a dough. Press into a tart tin. Put in the fridge and let it set for about 2 hours.

TO MAKE THE FILLING: Blend all the ingredients until smooth, adding water, as needed. Spread gently into the bottom of your tart crust and then let it harden in the fridge for 30 to 60 minutes. Now top the tart off with all the berries, slice and serve!

Maple Pecan Pie

Ooooh, baby. My dad loves pecan pie so I decided I may as well try my hand at making a raw version for him. Success was reached! This is a very rich recipe so you won't need a big slice. Try it out for Thanksgiving or Christmas. Or, you know . . . any occasion. This pie deserves a celebration all on its own.

> Makes: 1 pie, 8 to 10 servings

CRUST
1 cup (100 g) raw pecans
1 cup (175 g) pitted dates

FILLING
1/2 cup (130 g) raw cashew butter
1/2 cup (118 ml) coconut oil
1 cup (175 g) pitted dates
1/2 teaspoon vanilla extract
1 tablespoon (20 g) pure maple syrup
1/2 cup (43 g) unsweetened shredded coconut
Pinch of salt

TOPPING
Whole raw pecans

TO MAKE THE CRUST: Pulse the pecans into powder in your food processor, then add the dates and keep processing until everything sticks together. Press into a pie dish and put in the fridge.

TO MAKE THE FILLING: Blend all the ingredients until smooth. Spread onto your crust and arrange the pecans on top. Put back in the fridge for 2 hours or overnight. Slice. Chomp.

Naked Fruit Tarts (Nut-free, Coconut-free, Fat-free)

The only ingredients in these tarts are fruit, fruit and more fruit.
You can eat as many as you want. Heck, have them for dinner! I did.

> Makes: 2 huge tarts

CRUST
1 cup (175 g) pitted Medjool dates

FILLING
1 cup (145 g) blueberries,
strawberries or raspberries
1/2 cup (88 g) pitted dates

TOPPING
More berries!

TO MAKE THE CRUST: Squish the dates into parchment paper-lined tart tins, forming a sticky "crust." ("Wow that is *so* simple, Emily!" "I know, right!?")

TO MAKE THE FILLING: Blend the berries and dates until smooth and thick. Scoop into your crusts, and then top off with more berries and nom it down!

Lemon Dream Pie with Pecans & Coconut Vanilla Whipped Cream

I brought this pie to a friend's birthday party and took home a plate that was licked clean. There is just something special about the flavor profile of lemons; their combination of freshness, tartness and sweetness has been perfected by nature, and you can taste it in this recipe.

> Makes: 1 pie, 8 servings

CRUST
1 cup (90 g) oats
1½ cups (263 g) pitted dates

FILLING
1¼ cups (183 g) raw cashews
Juice of 5 lemons
1 cup (175 g) pitted dates
2 tablespoons (30 ml) melted coconut oil

TOPPINGS
Coconut cream (page 207)
¼ cup (28 g) chopped raw pecans

TO MAKE THE CRUST: Process the oats into flour in your food processor, then add the dates and process until it becomes a coarse dough, sticking together when pressed. Press into the bottom of a pie dish and put in the fridge.

TO MAKE THE FILLING: Blend all the ingredients until smooth. Spread evenly into your crust. Spread the coconut cream evenly over your pie and put back in the fridge, letting it set overnight. Then sprinkle with chopped pecans. Yum!

Rhubarb Almond Crumble with Maple Oregano Glaze

I was a little anxious about attempting to use raw rhubarb in a dessert, but I couldn't have been more pleased with the outcome. When you let it marinate in some kind of sweetener overnight, it becomes softer, sweeter and absolutely delicious. My original plan for the rhubarb was a tart, but I thought a deconstructed crumble would be more fun. I think the flavor combinations in this recipe are divine, but you should decide for yourself. This would be lovely to clean your palate after a healthy meal, along with some chilled white wine (or perhaps a maple oregano cocktail to match?)

> Makes: 5 to 6 servings

RHUBARB LAYER
About 1/2 pound (240 g) rhubarb
1/4 cup (85 g) pure maple syrup or other liquid sweetener
Handful fresh oregano leaves, finely chopped

CRUMBLE LAYER
2/3 cup (97 g) raw almonds
2/3 cup (117 g) pitted dates
1/2 teaspoon vanilla extract
1/2 teaspoon ground cinnamon

TO PREPARE THE RHUBARB: Slice each stalk in half, lengthwise. Cover in a shallow dish with the maple syrup and oregano. You can either put this in your oven at its lowest temperature for several hours and then set aside in a warm spot overnight, or use a dehydrator. This should cause the rhubarb to become much softer, sweeter and shrink. You should also have a pool of maple syrup and oregano leaves in your container by the time your rhubarb is done—this is your glaze. Chop the rhubarb into small pieces and set aside.

TO MAKE THE CRUMBLE: Pulse the almonds into flour in your food processor, add the rest of the ingredients and process until it begins to stick together. Press the crumble mixture into the bottom of cookie cutter molds and gently top them off with the rhubarb chunks, pressing everything down so it holds together inside the mold. Then carefully lift off the mold, revealing a cute little tower of crumble and rhubarb. Drizzle with your glaze and enjoy!

Peaceful Peach Cobbler

Although it doesn't meet the strict definition of a cobbler, it puts your mind in the right place for what kind of recipe to expect. This cobbler is more like a peach crumble in the form of a pie and so far I've never gotten a complaint. All I've done is take out the ingredients that don't make me happy (such as dairy, white flour and bleached sugar). This is best eaten the day it's made because the filling is simply sliced peaches, so it's the perfect recipe for a garden or summer party. Enjoy!

> Makes: 1 pie, 8 messy servings

CRUST AND TOPPING
1½ cups (218 g) raw almonds
1½ cups (263 g) pitted dates
Ground cinnamon
Ground nutmeg

FILLING
4 to 6 ripe peaches

TO MAKE THE CRUST: Pulse 1 cup (145 g) of the almonds in your food processor until they turn into flour, add 1 cup (175 g) of the dates and a bit of cinnamon and nutmeg. Press this into the bottom and sides of a pie dish. Process the remaining almonds and dates into a crumbly mixture.

Pit and slice the peaches into cubes or however you want them. Fill up your piecrust with them, and then sprinkle on your crumble. Slice as cleanly as possible, serve, smile.

Chocolate Banana Cream Pie

I remember making this recipe for the first time and then tasting it with the family after dinner . . . we all flipped out.

> Makes: 1 pie, 10 to 12 servings

CRUST
1 cup (145 g) raw pecans
1 cup (100 g) raw walnuts
1 ½ cups (175 g) pitted dates or 1 cup (145 g) raisins
Pinch of salt
½ teaspoon vanilla extract

FILLING
3 bananas
¼ cup (64 g) raw cashew butter
2 tablespoons (30 ml) melted coconut oil
¼ cup (85 g) pure maple syrup
¼ cup (59 ml) vegan milk (use as little as possible)
1 teaspoon vanilla extract
¼ cup (30 g) cacao powder
Pinch of salt

COCONUT WHIPPED CREAM
1 (14-ounce [400-ml]) can full-fat coconut milk, refrigerated for 48 hours
⅛ teaspoon stevia or powdered raw sugar
Seeds from 1 vanilla pod

TO MAKE THE CRUST: Pulse the nuts in your food processor into very small crumbs and add the dates and the rest of the crust ingredients. Process until it all sticks together. Press into a pie dish and put in the freezer.

TO MAKE THE FILLING: Blend all the ingredients—except for 1 banana—until smooth, then let it set and thicken in the fridge. When it is thick, enough, spoon into the piecrust, slice the remaining banana and layer on top and then put in the fridge.

TO MAKE THE COCONUT WHIPPED CREAM: After your coconut milk has chilled in the fridge, there should be a layer of solid coconut fat on top when you open the can; scoop this off and put into a chilled mixing bowl, then whip until stiff peaks form, adding the vanilla seeds and sweetener, as you like. Spread this all over your pie and let it set in the fridge for a few hours. Or devour it right away.

Almond Ginger Rosemary Tart with Coconut, Chia & Almond Caramel

Oooh baby! This is a quick, clean and easy recipe to throw together in an afternoon and enjoy the same day for dessert. I love the combination of almonds with coconut, ginger and rosemary—so in this recipe I put them all together, along with some sweet chia coconut pudding for the filling. If that doesn't sound delicious enough, drizzle anything with this almond caramel and it will become irresistible. Of course, any nuts will work for this recipe, not just almonds—it is up to your taste buds to decide.

> Makes: 1 small tart, about 4 servings

CRUST
³/₄ cup (109 g) raw almonds
³/₄ cup (132 g) pitted dates
1 tablespoon (8 g) grated fresh ginger
Small handful rosemary leaves

FILLING
2 tablespoons (21 g) chia seeds
1 tablespoon (20 g) preferred liquid sweetener
4 to 5 tablespoons (60 to 75 ml) water
2 tablespoons (11 g) unsweetened shredded coconut
1 tablespoon (16 g) raw almond butter

ALMOND CARAMEL
1 tablespoon (15 ml) raw almond butter
1 tablespoon (20 g) pure maple syrup
1 tablespoon (15 ml) melted coconut oil

TOPPINGS
Almonds
Fresh rosemary leaves
Unsweetened shredded coconut

TO MAKE THE CRUST: Pulse the almonds into flour in your food processor, then add the rest of the ingredients and process until it begins to stick together. Press into the bottom and up the sides of a small springform pan (mine is 4¹/₂ inches [11.5 cm] in diameter) and put in the fridge.

TO MAKE THE FILLING: Stir together all the ingredients and set aside for a few minutes, until the chia seeds have gelled and thickened the mixture. Spread evenly into your crust and put back in the fridge for 1 or 2 hours, until set.

TO MAKE THE CARAMEL: Stir together all the ingredients until smooth. Let it thicken by leaving it in the fridge for about 30 minutes (the coconut oil needs to resolidify).

ASSEMBLY: Take your tart out of the pan and put on a plate. Sprinkle with the toppings and drizzle with the caramel. Slice and enjoy.

Fresh Berry Tarts with Whipped Vanilla Coconut Cream

I absolutely adored whipped cream with fresh berries when I was younger and before I was vegan. When I chose to take dairy out of my diet, I was pretty bummed to say "bye" to the deliciously sweet combination. But then I discovered whipped coconut cream. It is honestly way better than the dairy version because it tastes like coconut, and is loads healthier. Although strictly speaking it is not raw, it's without a doubt still worth making. These would be perfect for a summer party outdoors, and are fun for everyone to make. Enjoy the simple delights nature provides.

> Makes: 4 tarts

CRUST
½ cup (135 g) raw hazelnuts
½ cup (73 g) raw almonds
1 cup (175 g) pitted dates
½ teaspoon vanilla extract

VANILLA COCONUT CREAM
1 (14-ounce [400-ml]) can full-fat coconut milk, refrigerated for 48 hours
Seeds from 1 vanilla pod
Pinch of stevia or raw sugar

TOPPING
Fresh, local, organic berries!

TO MAKE THE CRUST: Pulse the nuts into flour in your food processor, then add the dates and vanilla and process until a crumbly dough is formed. Press into parchment paper-lined tart tins and put in the fridge.

TO MAKE THE COCONUT CREAM: After your coconut milk has chilled in the fridge, there should be a layer of solid coconut fat on top when you open the can; scoop this off and put into a chilled mixing bowl, then whip until stiff peaks form, adding the vanilla seeds and sweetener, as you like.

Spread the whipped cream into your tart crusts and top off with your berries.

Banana Tart with Chocolate Cream, Jungle Peanut Butter & Candied Ginger Slices

Oh man; this guy's a keeper. The richness from the peanut butter, chocolate and bananas all mixed with the crumbly crust and finally topped off with the strong flavors of the ginger creates one wonderful bite. You can use whatever nut butter you like (I bet tahini would be mind-blowingly tasty) but I love the classic combination of chocolate and peanut butter . . . even if it is raw jungle peanut butter. I find jungle peanut butter to have a more bitter taste but it's really quite delicious when you get used to it. Nothing else to say about this recipe— except that you should make it right now!

> Makes: 1 tart, 8 to 10 servings

CRUST
1 cup (145 g) raw almonds
1¹/₂ cups (218 g) golden raisins

CHOCOLATE LAYER
¹/₄ cup (59 ml) melted coconut oil
¹/₃ cup (40 g) cacao powder
1 teaspoon vanilla extract
1 to 2 tablespoons (15 to 30 ml)
vegan milk or water

LAYERS
2 bananas, sliced
¹/₂ cup (130 g) jungle peanut butter
¹/₂ cup (56 g) ginger, sliced
Agave syrup, for coating

MAKE THE CRUST: Pulse the almonds in your food processor until they become a coarse flour, then add the raisins and process until it all begins to stick together. Press into a tart tin and put in the fridge.

MAKE THE CHOCOLATE LAYER: Mix all the ingredients together until smooth.

ASSEMBLY: Layer the banana slices onto your tart, then evenly spread with the peanut butter, followed by the chocolate. Coat the ginger slices in the agave and place decoratively on top. Let it set in the fridge for an hour or so, then slice and enjoy!

Chia Caramel Pecan Pie with Cinnamon Chocolate Sauce

What a wonderful world we live in, where we get to eat this pie.

> Makes: 1 pie, 8 to 10 servings

CRUST

2 cups (290 g) raw nuts or buckwheat flour

1 cup (175 g) pitted dates or prunes

1/2 teaspoon salt

FILLING

1/2 cup (88 g) pitted dates

1/4 cup (59 ml) melted coconut oil

6 tablespoons (62 g) chia seeds mixed with 3/4 cup (177 ml) water

1/2 teaspoon vanilla extract

1/2 teaspoon ground cinnamon

1 1/2 cups (218 g) raisins

Water

TOPPINGS (OPTIONAL)

Raw pecans

Raw pumpkin seeds

CINNAMON CHOCOLATE SAUCE

1 tablespoon (8 g) cacao powder

1 tablespoon (16 g) raw nut butter or melted coconut oil

1 tablespoon (20 g) pure maple syrup

1/2 teaspoon ground cinnamon

TO MAKE THE CRUST: Pulse the nuts in your food processor until they are crumb size. Add the dates and salt and process until it sticks together. Press into the bottom of a tart plate. Put in fridge.

TO MAKE THE FILLING: Process all ingredients—except 1/2 cup of the raisins—until smooth, adding water if needed. It will taste as if a divine entity has landed in your mouth. Stir in the reserved 1/2 cup of raisins by hand and pour into your crust. Let it set in the fridge for 3 hours (or overnight), then decorate with pecans, pumpkin seeds and chocolate sauce. Or not.

TO MAKE THE CHOCOLATE SAUCE: Mix all ingredients together until smooth. Drizzle onto your pie.

Fresh Citrus Tart with Lemon Cream

Perfect for summer, this is a refreshing, juicy, sweet tart layered with sliced grapefruit, orange and lime on a smooth lemon cream. I imagine this being eaten in a grassy meadow on a sunny day, with iced drinks and flowers nearby. You can use whatever fruit you like, but I wanted to keep a citrus theme throughout the recipe. I suggest using Meyer lemons for the lemon cream because they have a hint more sweetness than the regular kind.

> Makes: 1 tart, 8 to 10 servings

CRUST
1½ cups (135 g) oats
1½ cups (263 g) pitted dates

LEMON CREAM
1 cup (145 g) raw cashews
Juice of 2 lemons
2 tablespoons (40 g) pure maple syrup
1 tablespoon (15 ml) melted coconut oil

CITRUS LAYER
1 grapefruit
1 orange
1 lime or lemon

TO MAKE THE CRUST: Pulse the oats in your food processor until they become a coarse flour. Add the dates and process until it sticks together. Press into the bottom of tart dish and put in the fridge.

TO MAKE THE LEMON CREAM: Blend all the ingredients until smooth. Spread evenly into the bottom of your crust and put back in the fridge for about 1 hour.

Peel the citrus fruits and slice them how you like, then layer in the tart and sprinkle with lemon or orange zest. Enjoy.

Oversized Oreo Tart with Vanilla Coconut Cream & Chocolate Ganache

Holy *moly*. I'm sure you thought that a person cannot be happy all the time. Well, you are wrong; if you constantly have this tart around, you will never be sad again. I bet this would be adorable if you decorated it with raw Oroos (page 121).

> Makes: 1 tart, 10 to 12 servings

CRUST
1½ cups (150 g) raw walnuts
1½ cups (263 g) pitted dates
2 tablespoons (15 g) cacao powder

VANILLA COCONUT CREAM
1 cup (80 g) fresh young coconut meat
1 cup (145 g) raw cashews
3 tablespoons (60 g) preferred liquid sweetener
Coconut water or other liquid, use as little as possible
Seeds from 1 vanilla pod

CHOCOLATE GANACHE
2 avocados, peeled and pitted
3 tablespoons (45 ml) melted coconut oil
3 tablespoons (60 g) preferred liquid sweetener, or ½ cup (88 g) pitted dates
2 heaping tablespoons (18 g) cacao powder
1 teaspoon vanilla extract

Unsweetened shredded coconut, for sprinkling
Cacao nibs, for sprinkling

TO MAKE THE CRUST: Pulse the nuts into flour in your food processor, then add the dates and cacao and process until they stick together. Press into a tart tin and put in the fridge.

TO MAKE THE VANILLA COCONUT CREAM: Blend all the ingredients until smooth and very thick. You can add some coconut oil to help it solidify, if you like. Spread into the bottom of your tart crust and put back in the fridge.

TO MAKE THE CHOCOLATE GANACHE: Blend all the ingredients until smooth and creamy. It should be fairly thick but it will thicken more because of the coconut oil. Spread on top of your vanilla coconut cream and let it set in the fridge for a few hours. Sprinkle with coconut and cacao nibs, cut and nom it down!

Harvest Pumpkin Pie

This was one of the first raw pies I ever made, and I was so pleased with it that I made it a second time and brought it to a raw potluck downtown. Needless to say, the pie dish was empty by the end of the evening. This pie is perfect for winter holiday dinners, or any time local pumpkins are ripe for eating. Serve with coconut whipped cream (page 207) or raw ice cream (page 196) for extra decadence.

> Makes: 1 pie, 8 servings

CRUST

1 cup (145 g) raw cashews
1 cup (145 g) raw almonds
1 cup (175 g) pitted dates
¼ cup (35 g) raisins
⅛ teaspoon salt

PUMPKIN FILLING

1 peeled, seeded and cubed sugar pumpkin (about 7 cups [812 g])
1 cup (175 g) pitted dates
4 to 5 tablespoons (60 to 75 ml) melted coconut oil
⅓ cup (115 g) pure maple syrup
Ground cinnamon, nutmeg, ginger and cloves, for flavoring

TO MAKE THE CRUST: Pulse the nuts in your food processor until they are a coarse flour. Add the dates, raisins and salt. Pulse until it all sticks together in a ball. Press into the bottom of a pie dish and refrigerate.

TO MAKE THE PIE FILLING: Process the pumpkin cubes as much as possible in your food processor. Add the other ingredients, adding the spices to taste, and process until it can't get any smoother. Transfer the filling to your high-speed blender and blend on the highest setting to get it super smooth like the cooked version. Taste and add whatever else you think it needs. Spread the filling onto your piecrust and let it set in the fridge overnight.

Into the Wild Caramel Tarts with Pistachios, Pumpkin Seeds & Chocolate Trees

I got the inspiration for these from a drawing by Marc Johns called *I Have a Crush on Trees*. It's just adorable; you should Google it to see what I mean. From there, I basically decided to make each tart look like a—very simplified—miniature forest. The crust and caramel filling are meant to be the ground, the pistachios and pumpkin seeds are the grass, and the chocolate trees are . . . well, trees. For this recipe, homemade raw chocolate can be tricky to make the trees with because it isn't as solid at room temperature, so you may want to simply buy a bar of raw or dark chocolate for that.

> Makes: 3 large tarts

CRUST
1 cup (145 g) raw almonds
1 cup (175 g) pitted dates

FILLING
¾ cup (132 g) pitted dates
2 tablespoons (30 ml) melted coconut oil
1 tablespoon (16 g) raw almond butter
1 to 2 tablespoons (15 to 30 ml) water
Pinch of salt (optional)

TOPPING
¼ cup (59 ml) liquid raw chocolate (page 209)
2 tablespoons (18 g) chopped raw pistachios
2 tablespoons (17 g) chopped raw pumpkin seeds

TO MAKE THE CRUST: Pulse the almonds into flour in your food processor, then add the dates and process until they begin to stick together. Press into the bottom of tart tins and put in the fridge.

TO MAKE THE FILLING: Blend the ingredients until very smooth and thick. Spread into your tart crusts and put back in the fridge.

TO MAKE THE CHOCOLATE TREES: Fill a piping bag with the melted chocolate and then carefully pipe your trees onto parchment paper. Put the parchment paper in the freezer for a few minutes, until the trees are hardened. Sprinkle the chopped nuts onto your tarts, and then stick in your trees. If they fall over, just stack up some nuts right behind the "stumps" to hold them in place. Voilà!

Banana Ice-Cream Tarts with Salted Nutmeg Caramel

Bliss! Banana bliss, that is. The crust of these tastes like butter tarts (a beloved Canadian pastry) and the filling is like banana bread ice cream. Need I say more? The answer is no.

> Makes: 4 large tarts

CRUST
1 cup (145 g) raw pecans
1 cup (145 g) raisins

CARAMEL
1/2 cup (88 g) pitted dates barely covered in water
Salt (optional)
1/2 teaspoon ground nutmeg
1 tablespoon (15 ml) melted coconut oil
Water

ICE CREAM
1 banana, frozen
1/2 teaspoon ground cinnamon
1/2 teaspoon vanilla powder

TO MAKE THE CRUST: Pulse the pecans into flour in your food processor. Add the raisins and process until they stick together. Press into tart molds and put in the fridge.

TO MAKE THE CARAMEL: Blend all the ingredients until smooth, adding water, as needed.

TO MAKE THE ICE CREAM: Cut up the banana, then throw the pieces into your blender along with the cinnamon and vanilla, and blend until very thick, white and creamy—it's just like soft-serve! It will take just seconds, you may have to stop your blender and push the banana down into the blades so it can blend fully. Now fill your tart crusts with the ice cream and spoon on your caramel. Eat right away because the banana ice cream melts über fast!

Strawberries 'n' Cream Tartlets

Can't go wrong with strawberries and cream!

> Makes: about 4 mini tarts

CRUST
1 cup (145 g) raw pecans
1 cup (175 g) pitted dates

CREAM
1 cup (145 g) raw cashews
2 tablespoons (30 ml) melted coconut oil
1 tablespoon (20 g) preferred liquid sweetener
Juice of 1 lemon
1 teaspoon vanilla extract
Water (optional)

TOPPING
Strawberries, hulled and sliced
Dried coconut, finely ground

TO MAKE THE CRUST: Pulse the pecans into flour in your food processor, then add the dates and process until everything begins to stick together. Press into tart molds and put in the fridge.

TO MAKE THE CREAM: Blend all the ingredients until smooth and thick, adding water, if needed. Spread into your tart crusts and refrigerate overnight. The next day, top off with sliced strawberries and coconut and enjoy!

Boston Banana Cream Deep Dish Tarts

These were created through a series of improvisations when I was featured on an episode of *Sylvia's Vegan Kitchen*. The recipe was meant to be something like an Oreo tart (page 159), but some things went wrong—or maybe they went right?—and we wound up with these. I do not regret it! I remade them at home and tweaked the recipe. Your first thought after you bite into them will be probably be, "No way. These are *way* too good to be good *for* me." But then you'll remember that all you used to make them was avocado, cacao, banana, dates and nuts. Yep. The world is awesome.

> Makes: 4 huge tarts

CRUST
1 cup (145 g) raw nuts
1 cup (175 g) raisins or pitted dates
1 teaspoon cacao powder

CHOCOLATE PUDDING
1 avocado, peeled and pitted
1 tablespoon (15 ml) melted coconut oil
1 tablespoon (8 g) cacao powder
4 to 5 dates, pitted, or 1 tablespoon (20 g) preferred liquid sweetener
Water (optional)

BANANA CREAM
1 banana, mashed until smooth

TO MAKE THE CRUST: Pulse the nuts into flour in your food processor. Add the raisins and cacao, and process until it begins to stick together. Press into the bottom and sides of large, parchment paper–lined cupcake tins and put in the fridge.

TO MAKE THE CHOCOLATE PUDDING: Blend all the ingredients until smooth. If it's too thick, add a tiny bit of water. Using half of your pudding, scoop a bit into the bottom of each of your tart crusts, making a little indentation in the middle to put the banana cream; scoop in a spoonful of banana cream into each indentation and then cover up with the rest of your chocolate pudding. Let them set in the fridge for an hour or two, then nom away.

chapter 4

Pudding & Ice Cream

THE FIRST TIME I HAD AVOCADO CHOCOLATE PUDDING, I just about fell off my chair—in a good way. I could not believe how good it tasted and I probably inhaled the entire bowl right where I was (tentatively) sitting. The bases for my pudding recipes are usually from avocados, bananas or chia seeds, because they allow the result to be so smooth, and they also all have their own unique flavor and texture profiles. If you don't like the flavor of or are allergic to any of them, you can substitute another. No biggie. These puddings are best eaten right away, but if you keep them in the fridge for a couple of days, they should still be fine. Personally speaking, there is never any leftover pudding in my house . . . that is because I eat it all.

I scream for raw, dairy-free ice cream! Okay, that doesn't have quite the same ring to it, but it is true nonetheless. I really do love these ice cream recipes . . . maybe a little too much? Nah. No such thing. I'd say these are great for eating in hot weather but they are actually perfect for any time of year. I remember when I first became vegan, I was deeply saddened that I was giving up ice cream, because it is one of my favorite treats. Then I learned of the world of vegan ice cream—skies brightened. Shortly after, I discovered the world of *raw* vegan ice cream—angels sang. Needless to say, you do not have to be sad about giving up ice cream if you go vegan. You are exposed to a whole new universe of sweet, dairy-free frozen magic and I personally have never looked back.

Amazing Avocado Chocolate Pudding

Now you can eat chocolate pudding for breakfast. You're welcome.

> Makes: 2 to 4 servings

2 avocados, peeled and pitted

2 tablespoons (15 g) cacao powder

2 to 3 tablespoons (40 to 60 g) preferred liquid sweetener, or ½ cup (88 g) pitted dates

½ teaspoon vanilla extract

Pinch of ground cinnamon, salt and/or cayenne pepper (optional)

Almond milk

Blend everything until smooth and thick, adding almond milk, as needed, to make it creamy.

Cacao Carob Vanilla Towers with Macadamias & Chocolate Walnut Garnish

Om nom nom. These are delicious and I am pretty sure that if you think otherwise, you're crazy. Chocolate on carob on vanilla: what is not to love, exactly? You can make these in any shape you want; they don't have to be tall towers. I simply like the aesthetics of some being tall, but if you don't have the right molds to do this, it can be time consuming so just go with whatever mold or cookie cutter you feel like. Break the mold (figuratively speaking) and make 'em short and fat! No matter what dimension, they are gonna taste great.

> Makes: 4

CACAO LAYER
¾ cup (132 g) pitted dates
1 tablespoon (15 ml) melted coconut oil
Pinch of salt (optional)
2 tablespoons (30 ml) water, or as needed
1 heaping tablespoon (9 g) cacao powder

CAROB LAYER
¾ cup (75 g) raw walnuts
1 tablespoon (15 ml) melted coconut oil
1 to 2 tablespoons (20 to 40 g) pure maple syrup
½ tablespoon (4 g) carob powder
2 tablespoons (30 ml) water, or as needed

VANILLA LAYER
¾ cup (101 g) raw macadamia nuts
1 to 2 tablespoons (20 to 40 g) pure maple syrup
1 tablespoon (15 ml) melted coconut oil
1 to 2 tablespoons (15 to 30 ml) water

CHOCOLATE WALNUT GARNISH (OPTIONAL)
¼ cup (25 g) raw walnuts
¼ cup (59 ml) liquid raw chocolate (page 209)

TO MAKE EACH LAYER: Simply blend the according ingredients until smooth and layer them in molds, in the order given. Put in the fridge or freezer overnight until set.

TO MAKE THE GARNISH: Cover the walnuts with the chocolate and then—depending on how many towers you made—form a few clusters of chocolate-covered walnuts. When the chocolate hardens, the clusters should stick together. When your towers are set, take them out of their molds, place a garnish on top of each one and enjoy!

Breakfast Parfaits with Layers of Fruit & Chia Pudding

This is a simple recipe that requires no equipment and hardly any time. I love chia seeds because they are nutrition powerhouses full of protein, fiber, amino acids, calcium, vitamin C, potassium and omega-3s. They are terrific for your hair and skin and are great at helping balance blood sugar levels. And yes—they are the same seeds that grow those infamous "Chia pets." You can serve this in a bowl or glass, whatever floats your boat.

> Makes: 1 serving

CHIA PUDDING

1 tablespoon (10 g) chia seeds

1/4 cup (59 ml) water

1 tablespoon (20 g) pure maple syrup

1/2 teaspoon ground cinnamon

FRUIT LAYERS

1/3 cup (52 g) pitted cherries

1/3 cup (49 g) blueberries

1/3 cup (42 g) raspberries

1/3 cup (52 g) chopped pineapple

MAKE THE PUDDING: Mix the chia seeds with the water and other ingredients. The chia seeds will quickly turn the mixture into a gel-like consistency.

ASSEMBLY: Layer the fruit with the chia pudding and eat with a fork or spoon.

Chia Vanilla Pudding with Cinnamon & Raisins

This is a delightfully healthy recipe that can be eaten as a meal for breakfast, lunch or dinner, or a simple snack any time of the day. I remember loving rice pudding when I was younger, and wanted to make an easy raw version. Of course, this isn't really like rice pudding at all, but I'd take this over the original any day. I think this recipe tastes best cold.

> Makes: 2 to 4 servings

¼ cup (145 g) raw almonds

¾ cup (177 ml) water, or as needed

¼ cup (175 g) pitted dates

2 tablespoons (21 g) chia seeds

½ teaspoon ground cinnamon, or to taste

2½ tablespoons (23 g) raisins

Blend the almonds, water and dates together until smooth and creamy. At this point you want a thick, sweet, nut milk kind of mixture. Add the chia seeds, cinnamon and raisins and put in the fridge for about an hour so the chia can absorb the liquid. Adjust according to taste, then sprinkle with your desired toppings, such as chopped nuts, more raisins and cinnamon, berries, etc.

Crème Brûlée of Cashews, Coconut, Lavender & Cinnamon with Banana Layers

This is a lovely-looking and fun-to-make recipe that is equally delightful to eat. Its smooth, light creaminess and refreshing hints of lavender make a truly blissful tasting experience. The "brûlée" layer is simply sweetened coconut oil stirred with cinnamon to create a hard casing for the cashew pudding underneath. Banana always works well with nutty flavors, and as the base of the pudding is cashews, I think the layered banana slices pair perfectly.

> Makes: 4 servings

PUDDING

1 cup (145 g) raw cashews

3 tablespoons (60 g) pure maple syrup

½ banana

Seeds from 1 vanilla pod, or 1 teaspoon vanilla extract

1 teaspoon dried food-grade lavender flowers

2 to 3 tablespoons (30 to 45 ml) melted coconut oil

LAYERS

½ banana, thinly sliced

TOP LAYER

3 tablespoons (45 ml) melted coconut oil

1 teaspoon ground cinnamon

1 tablespoon (20 g) pure maple syrup

TO MAKE THE PUDDING: Blend all the ingredients until smooth (it should be thick and creamy), and then fill up four small bowls a little less than halfway. Layer with half of your banana slices. Pour the remaining pudding over this and layer with the rest of the banana slices.

TO MAKE THE TOP LAYER: Mix the ingredients until fully combined then pour over your puddings and put in the fridge until the top layers have hardened. Enjoy with spoons and flowers.

Coffee Crème Mousse with Chocolate Pecan Crust

I made these for Mother's Day because the day before, my mom had mentioned this Irish coffee and chocolate cake recipe she saw on the Internet, and how sinfully good she thought it looked . . . challenge accepted. I don't drink coffee, but put it in a dessert and I will be licking the plate clean. I think this recipe turned out perfect, and my mom agreed (which is the most important thing, right?). Remember to buy fair trade, organic coffee beans!

> Makes: 4 to 8 servings

CRUST
¾ cup (75 g) raw pecans
1 heaping tablespoon (9 g) cacao powder
¾ cup (132 g) pitted dates
Pinch of salt

COFFEE CRÈME
½ cup (118 ml) strong brewed coffee, or as needed
¾ cup (109 g) raw cashews
1 cup (175 g) pitted dates
1 teaspoon vanilla extract
1 tablespoon (15 ml) melted coconut oil

CHOCOLATE TOPPING
¼ cup (59 ml) melted coconut oil
¼ cup (85 g) pure maple syrup
⅓ cup (40 g) cacao powder
Pinch of salt

4 raw pecans, for garnish

TO MAKE THE CRUST: Pulse the pecans in your food processor until they become a coarse flour, add the remaining ingredients and process until it begins to clump together. Press into the bottom of large lined cupcake tins, or your preferred molds. Put in the fridge.

TO MAKE THE COFFEE CRÈME: Blend all the ingredients until smooth and pretty thick, adding as much coffee as you need to make it creamy—but don't add too much because then it won't set. Spread onto your crusts and put back in the fridge, preferably overnight.

TO MAKE THE CHOCOLATE TOPPING: Mix all the ingredients until smooth and then spread thinly on parchment paper. Put in the fridge or freezer until it solidifies. Cut into small pieces and sprinkle on your cupcakes. Top off each with a pecan. Eat.

Rawky Road Ice Cream with Marshmallow & Chocolate Chunks

Oh my gosh oh my gosh oh my gosh oh my gosh.

> Makes: 1 mega serving

3 bananas, frozen
1 tablespoon (8 g) cacao powder
1 s'more cupcake (page 36)

Blend the bananas until they become like soft-serve ice cream (it'll take just a minute and then change suddenly), then add the cacao and blend until combined. Scoop into a bowl. Break up the s'more cupcake and crumble it on top of your ice cream. You know what to do next.

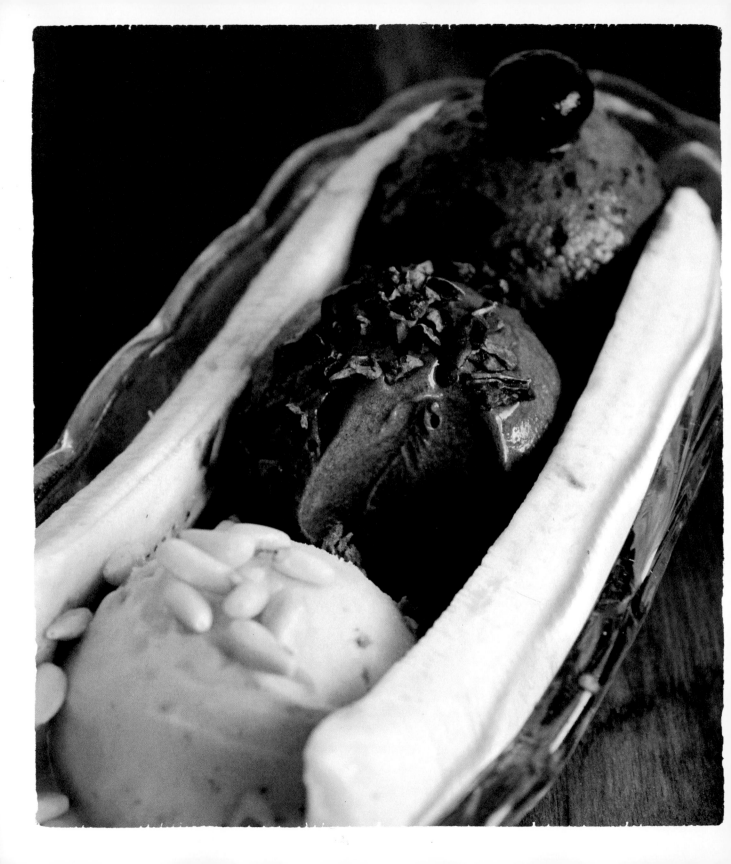

The Real Banana Split

Three different kinds (banana, berry and chocolate) of banana soft-serve ice cream sprinkled with superfoods and served with a split banana—I know I always say this, but it really doesn't get better! Another plus is that this sweet, creamy frozen dessert can be your breakfast because it takes only a moment to make and is basically just three bananas. I know, right!? Heaven on earth.

> Makes: 1 mega banana split

2 bananas, frozen
1 teaspoon cacao powder
¼ cup (64 g) frozen berries
1 fresh banana

Blend the frozen bananas into ice cream in your blender or food processor. Take out two-thirds of the ice cream and set aside. Add the cacao to the remaining ice cream in the machine and blend until combined. Scoop this into a bowl. Put half of your leftover ice cream back into the machine along with the berries, and blend until you get berry ice cream; scoop into the bowl with the chocolate. Your remaining ice cream is simply banana ice cream! Add it to your bowl, slice the fresh banana and serve it with your ice cream. Feel free to sprinkle on such toppings as cacao nibs, nuts and berries.

Ice-Cream Sandwiches with Rosemary Almond Cookies & Berry Medley Ice Cream

I could eat all of these in one sitting, no kidding. This recipe has four ingredients (or five if you add rosemary). I love how simple and filling raw desserts are: there are no lame filler ingredients, such as flour, baking soda and sugar. Every single component of these recipes is a whole food, special and delicious on its own. You wouldn't snack on flour while baking, would you? Or grab a few tablespoons of sugar when making ice cream, right? Those ingredients are too refined to be good on their own. In my recipes, I like using only foods that are awesome all by themselves. Get messy with these bad boys.

> Makes: 6 to 8 sandwiches with scraps left over

ROSEMARY ALMOND COOKIES
1 cup (145 g) raw almonds
1 cup (175 g) pitted dates
A few fresh rosemary leaves

BERRY ICE CREAM
2 bananas, frozen
1 cup (255 g) frozen strawberries

TO MAKE THE COOKIES: Process all the ingredients in your food processor until they stick together. Press half of this cookie mixture into the bottom of a parchment paper-lined baking pan, so it ends up being about ³/₈ inch (1 cm) thick, or however thick you want your cookies to be! Put in the fridge.

TO MAKE THE ICE CREAM: Put the fruit into your high-speed blender and blend for several minutes, continuing to push the fruit into the blades. In just a moment, the frozen fruit chunks will turn into a creamy thick soft-serve ice cream. Spread this onto your bottom cookie layer and put it back in the freezer until it's solid. Then press the rest of your cookie mixture on top. Again, put in the freezer until totally solid. Cut out cookies with . . . cookie cutters (duh). Nom nom nom!

Banana Ice Cream, The Best Thing Ever

The title says it all.

> Makes: 1 serving

3 bananas, frozen

Put the bananas into your high-speed blender and blend; keep pushing the bananas down into the blades, it will take just a moment and suddenly you will have a magically creamy, smooth, white, soft-serve ice cream. You can also add dates, nut butter, fruit or cacao powder to take this baby to the next level.

Chocolate & Vanilla Ice-Cream Sandwiches

Why would anyone want a normal ice-cream sandwich when you can eat this super awesome one? Try making them and see what I mean.

> Makes: 8 to 10 servings

CRUST

1 cup (170 g) buckwheat groats, soaked in water for 1 to 3 hours

¼ cup (30 g) cacao powder

¼ cup (35 g) raw pumpkin seeds

½ teaspoon ground cinnamon

3 tablespoons (36 g) hemp seeds

1 cup (175 g) pitted dates

2 tablespoons (32 g) raw nut butter (optional)

Banana ice cream (page 191) or vanilla ginger ice cream (page 196)

TO MAKE THE CRUST: Pulse the dry ingredients in your food processor until it is a coarse flour. Add the rest of the ingredients and process until it forms a ball or clumps together.

Using half of the crust mixture, press into the bottom of cookie cutter molds or whatever else you want to use. Scoop softened ice cream into each one and then set in the freezer for an hour or so, until the ice cream is hard again. Press on the remaining half of the crust mixture. Let them set in the freezer for 30 more minutes and then push them gently out of the molds. Enjoy!

Strawberry Cheesecake Pops with Coconut Flakes

These will stop you in your tracks and make you say, "Oh my goodness." My friend said they taste like strawberry cheesecake, so that's what I named them. I'm logical like that.

> Makes: 10 pops

ICE CREAM

1 cup (80 g) fresh young coconut meat

1 cup (175 g) pitted dates

1 cup (145 g) raw cashews

1 cup (236 ml) coconut water or vegan milk

1 cup (145 g) hulled strawberries

Seeds from 1 vanilla pod

¼ cup (21 g) unsweetened shredded coconut

TO MAKE THE ICE CREAM: Blend all the ingredients until smooth. Pour into your pop molds and put in the freezer. When they are frozen solid, take them out of their molds (run hot water over the outside to help get them out), coat them in coconut, then nom them up!

Vanilla Ginger Ice-Cream Pops with Chocolate Coating

This is one of my favorite ice cream recipes because it's so simple yet insanely satisfying. Every bite leaves you wanting more. The ginger is optional and you can make it very subtle or the star flavor in the show—it's up to you as always. I like to experiment with different flavors and I have found that ginger pairs deliciously with vanilla. With or without it, this recipe is a winner. Don't be surprised if people ask for a second one.

> Makes: 10 pops

ICE CREAM

1 cup (80 g) fresh young coconut meat

1 cup (175 g) pitted dates

1 cup (145 g) raw cashews

1 cup (236 ml) coconut water or vegan milk

Seeds from 1 vanilla pod

Ground ginger, or grated fresh

CHOCOLATE COATING

3 tablespoons (45 ml) melted coconut oil

3 tablespoons (23 g) cacao powder

2 tablespoons (40 g) pure maple syrup

Pumpkin seeds, for garnish (optional)

Blend all the ingredients until smooth. Pour into your pop molds and put in the freezer. When they are frozen solid, take them out of their molds (run hot water over the outside to help get them out). Make the chocolate sauce by mixing all the ingredients together until smooth. Dip the pops in the liquid chocolate (and pumpkin seeds, if you'd like) and then gobble the goodness down.

Deconstructed Creamsicles with Orange and Vanilla Layers

Because these use only natural whole-food ingredients, they aren't bright orange and white like the store-bought kind, but I see this as a good thing: no mysterious food coloring required! These taste deliciously similar to my childhood memories of licking Creamsicles in the sunshine before they melted, and always asking hopefully for a second one. If you have pop molds that allow you to have an inner and outer layer, use those to get your recipe closer to the original; but I don't, so I'm keeping it simple. Let's get cool!

> Makes: 10 pops

ORANGE LAYER

2 peeled oranges

2½ tablespoons (50 g) pure maple syrup, or to taste

3 tablespoons (45 ml) melted coconut oil

VANILLA COCONUT LAYER

1 cup (80 g) fresh young coconut meat

1 cup (175 g) pitted dates

1 cup (145 g) raw cashews

1 cup (236 ml) coconut water, vegan milk or other liquid

Seeds from 1 vanilla pod

MAKE THE ORANGE LAYER: Blend all the ingredients together, then pour evenly into 10 pop molds; they should end up being about halfway full (I'm an optimist). Put these in your freezer at an angle so when they freeze the orange layer will be slanted and look all impressive.

MAKE THE VANILLA COCONUT LAYER: Blend all the ingredients together, then pour on top of your orange layer in each of your molds. Freeze until solid, then chow down!

Heavenly Banana Date Shake

This is the simplest and most delicious drink you will ever make. It's like a giant glass of creamy, frosty banana bread—the healthiest banana bread on the planet. You can use whatever nut butter you like, and feel free to add other spices, such as nutmeg. If you want to make this today but don't have any frozen bananas, simply cut two bananas into thin slices and put in the freezer on a plate; within two hours or so you'll be ready to roll.

> Makes: 1 shake

2 bananas, frozen
1 tablespoon (16 g) raw nut butter
$\frac{1}{2}$ teaspoon ground cinnamon
$\frac{1}{2}$ teaspoon vanilla powder
$\frac{1}{2}$ cup (118 ml) water or vegan milk
Handful of dates, pitted

Blend. Drink. Smile.

The Ultimate Chocolate Shake with Coconut Whipped Cream & Cacao Sprinkles

Honestly, who even wants to drink the milk of another species when you have this glorious dairy-free beauty to slurp. You can chug this thing feeling proud that you're getting in three servings of fruit as well as a whop of other high quality nutrients to keep you living long. Momma Nature does it again.

> Makes: 1 to 2 servings

SHAKE
3 bananas, frozen

1/4 cup (44 g) pitted dates

2 tablespoons (15 g) cacao powder

1 tablespoon (20 g) preferred liquid sweetener (optional)

1 tablespoon (16 g) raw almond butter

1 to 2 cups (236 to 473 ml) almond milk

1/2 teaspoon vanilla extract

Ground cinnamon or cayenne pepper (optional)

TOPPINGS
3 tablespoons (45 ml) coconut whipped cream (page 207)

1 teaspoon cacao nibs

Blend all the ingredients together until almost totally smooth. Feel free to add cinnamon or cayenne for extra flavor. Top off with coconut whipped cream and cacao nibs. Stick in a straw and smile. Oh yeah— then drink it.

Sorbet with Strawberries, Agave & Mint

Delightful and refreshing any time of the day.

> Makes: 1 serving

1 cup (255 g) frozen strawberries
1 teaspoon agave nectar (optional)
Sprig of fresh mint, for garnish

Blend the strawberries and agave into a smooth, creamy sorbet, then decorate with the mint and enjoy!

chapter 5

Basic Recipes

This short section has recipes that are used frequently in my desserts and I also give you a recipe for hot cacao because it *had* to be included. Enjoy!

Coconut Cream

You can buy full-fat canned coconut milk, refrigerate it for 48 hours and then scoop off the fat that has settled on top, to make whipped coconut cream if you want. It's delicious and I use it in a few of my recipes. But this version is 100 percent raw and has more pure coconut flavor. If you want the cream to be white, use a liquid sweetener, such as agave, but otherwise some dates will work just fine.

> Makes: about 2 cups (409 ml)

⅔ cup (54 g) fresh young coconut meat

½ cup (118 ml) coconut water, or as needed

¼ cup (41 g) raw cashews

2 tablespoons (40 g) preferred liquid sweetener

1 teaspoon freshly squeezed lemon juice

½ cup (118 ml) melted coconut oil

Blend all the ingredients until smooth, thick and creamy; you may have to chill it to make it thicker.

Raw Chocolate

You need this in your life.

> Makes: a little over 1 cup (180 g)

½ cup (60 g) cacao powder or carob powder

½ cup (118 ml) melted cacao butter or coconut oil

⅓ cup (115 g) preferred liquid sweetener

Mix all the ingredients together until smooth. Pour into chocolate molds or a parchment paper–lined baking sheet. Put in the fridge or freezer until solid. Optional additions: vanilla, chili powder, ground cinnamon, goji berries, hazelnuts, mesquite powder . . . the list goes on. This is merely a foundation recipe to make all your healthy chocolate dreams come true.

Date Paste

Nature's perfect sweetener. Use this to keep recipes 100 percent raw and wholesome.

> Makes: about 2 cups (477 ml)

1 cup (175 g) pitted dates
1 cup (236 ml) water
1 to 2 teaspoons freshly squeezed lemon juice

Blend until smooth; add more or less water for the desired consistency. Store in an airtight container in the fridge.

Hot Cacao

The Mayans were the original hot chocolate worshippers, creating a superfood blend of cacao, hot water, chile and sometimes vanilla thousands of years ago. It gave them strength and brain power and has done so for many civilizations since. This is why I trust cacao is great for me—read your history! Indulge in this sweet, decadent drink, knowing it will provide you with energy and high-quality nutrition.

> Makes: 1 cuppa hot cacao

1 cup (236 ml) water or vegan milk

1 tablespoon (8 g) cacao powder

1/8 teaspoon chili powder, or to taste

1/8 teaspoon vanilla extract

1 tablespoon (20 g) preferred liquid sweetener

1 tablespoon (15 ml) coconut oil

Heat the water until very warm. Blend with the rest of the ingredients until smooth and well combined. Taste and adjust the flavors accordingly.

Resources

Ingredients

As mentioned before, the majority of the ingredients you are going to see in these recipes are fresh and dried fruit, nuts, seeds and sometimes oats or buckwheat groats. Let's get down to specifics; I suggest having the following foods in your pantry or kitchen at all times, because they are the base of most of my recipes. You can buy them all online (preferably organic and raw—yeah, baby!) for reasonable prices. I suggest buying from Upaya Naturals if you live in Canada.

NUTS AND SEEDS: I usually have a variety on hand at any given time. Pecans, almonds, cashews, pine nuts, macadamias, walnuts, pistachios, pumpkin seeds, hemp seeds, flaxseeds, sunflower seeds . . . the list goes on. You can usually substitute any nut for any other nut, and the same goes for seeds. Nuts and seeds (along with oats and buckwheat groats) make up the "flour" component of raw desserts; they are the dry ingredients. They are high in protein, omega-3s (a healthy fat), fiber, zinc, magnesium, calcium, phosphorous, B vitamins and vitamin E. Additionally, they have been proven to lower the risk of heart disease and lower bad cholesterol levels while increasing good ones.

OATS AND BUCKWHEAT GROATS: Some people complain that raw desserts have too much fat because they're made of mostly nuts, so I make an effort to keep fat content at a minimum with my recipes—oats and buckwheat groats really help with this. Oats work excellently for crusts (in place of nuts) and if you prefer gluten-free, you can use buckwheat groats (or gluten-free oats). If you use gluten-free oats or buckwheat, it makes all my recipes gluten-free. Yippee!

DRIED FRUIT: For my recipes I use primarily dates, followed by raisins, prunes and figs. Medjool dates are best because they're very large and kinda gooey, but it's fun to experiment with different kinds. Dried fruits make up the sticky part of your raw desserts—along with coconut oil and liquid sweeteners, they are the wet ingredients. Dates and other dried fruits are a great source of cancer-fighting antioxidants, fiber, B vitamins, potassium and magnesium. These all help to improve brain function, balance blood sugar levels, strengthen bones and help reduce blood pressure. Yay for fruit! It's the perfect food.

LIQUID SWEETENERS: In my recipes, I let you choose which sweetener you want to use because there are several options. Generally you can use pure maple syrup, agave nectar, coconut nectar, raw honey (this is not vegan) or date paste (page 210). Technically, maple syrup is not raw, but you will only ever use liquid sweeteners in very small amounts and so this is hardly something to obsess over. Maple syrup is the sweetener I recommend because it is nutritious, vegan, and fairly unrefined, but you can decide for yourself what sweetener you like best after a little research and taste-testing. To each their own.

COCONUT OIL: Please, try to buy raw organic virgin coconut oil for maximum flavor and nutrition! It is excellent as a skin moisturizer as well (don't use it on your face, though. It'll clog your pores). Virtually all my recipes ask for *melted* coconut oil because it's naturally solid at room temperature, so you have to melt it yourself. To melt coconut oil: Put the required amount in a bowl and place this bowl over some steaming water until the coconut oil becomes liquid. Easy-peasy. Coconut oil plays a role in lowering bad cholesterol, boosting immunity, increasing metabolism, helping with weight loss, and it's also great for your hair and skin.

CACAO & CAROB: These guys are used for my chocolate recipes. Cacao is raw cocoa, and comes from the bean of the cacao tree. Its name means "food of the gods" in Nahuatl. You can get it in the form of powder or nibs; both are good to have for my recipes but I definitely use cacao powder more than cacao nibs; You can also buy cacao butter to use in raw chocolate, instead of coconut oil. Cacao has been shown to improve mood, brain function, blood circulation and enhance metabolism. It's rich in antioxidants, fiber, manganese, sulfur and magnesium. Carob comes from the pod of the carob tree, and is crushed to form carob powder. It has less fat and more sweetness than cacao and can be used as a substitute for cacao in all my recipes. Carob has antiviral, antibacterial, antiallergic properties and helps with digestion. It can play a role in regulating blood glucose and lowering cholesterol. Note: Carob is non-poisonous to dogs (unlike cacao), so if you want to make raw vegan chocolate puppy treats—or your dog likes to steal your desserts—use carob!

Equipment

Some people think that making raw food recipes requires a lot of expensive equipment—this isn't necessarily true. Yes, you can choose to spend a lot of money on every fancy appliance out there and this is great if you can afford it, but for my dessert recipes the most important piece of equipment you'll need is a good-quality food processor. I use one for almost every recipe in here. You can find excellent ones online for around $150; I recommend Cuisinart or KitchenAid. Other equipment you may want to consider purchasing to make my recipes are a blender and dehydrator. I recommend Vitamix blenders; they are rock stars in the kitchen, and I use mine every day to make green smoothies and a plethora of other healthful delights; Blendtec blenders are on the same level. They are a bit of an investment, but so worth it. Note: Most of my recipes that ask for a blender will also work if you just use a food processor, albeit they won't be as smooth—but I'm savin' ya money here! Last, we have dehydrators. They are set at low temperatures to gently dry your food over several hours. If you want to buy one, I suggest Excalibur—a pretty epic name—but I hardly ever dehydrate things, so you can just use your oven at its lowest temperature instead, if you don't mind. I often use my convection oven at its "keep warm" setting, and it works fine.

Substitutions, Adaptations & Allergies

As noted earlier, there are practically endless substitutions and variations you can try with raw food recipes. What you choose to use depends entirely on your preference. I want to give you as many options as possible because to me, the most important part of eating healthy is doing what works for you. Food is personal! Whether you want low-fat, gluten-free, coconut-free or nut-free recipes; I promise you will be able to find something that works, or else I'll eat my hat. Of course, I'm not wearing a hat—but you get the message.

Virtually all nuts are interchangeable, and the same goes for seeds. You can substitute oats for buckwheat groats, and vice versa. Dates, raisins, figs and prunes can all be substituted for each other. Cacao butter can be used in place of coconut oil. All liquid sweeteners are interchangeable. For my ice-cream cakes and cheesecakes, many people ask what they can use instead of bananas or nuts; I tell them that young coconut meat, dates and avocado do the job (and I ain't lyin'). Cacao and carob powder can be substituted for each other whenever you like.

Acknowledgments

I'd like to thank everyone at Page Street Publishing (especially Will, Marissa and Meg) for making this book happen. It's a dream come true.

I have to thank my parents for always accepting my weird ways and supporting whatever I do 100 percent; much love to you, Mom and Dad.

I am so grateful to every one of my caring and enthusiastic readers who have brought me to where I am at this moment—I could not have done this without your support.

Last, I need to give thanks to the universe (what a crazy connected place, right?) and *you!* You are the best.

About the Author

Emily von Euw lives near Vancouver in beautiful British Columbia, Canada. She spends her time hugging trees, punch-dancing to weird music, laughing with friends, contemplating dreams, attending university, working on her award-winning blog (www.thisrawsomeveganlife.com), doing spontaneous calf raises, consuming enormous amounts of raw chocolate and green juice and writing the occasional book. Oh, and she thinks you're really cool.

Index